PIZZAS
and FLATBREADS

OVER 100 RECIPES FEATURING EVERYONE'S FAVORITE COMFORT FOODS

13-Digit ISBN: 978-1-60433-836-2
10-Digit ISBN: 1-60433-836-9

This book may be ordered by mail from the publisher. Please include $5.99 for postage and handling. Please support your local bookseller first!

Books published by Cider Mill Press Book Publishers are available at special discounts for bulk purchases in the United States by corporations, institutions, and other organizations. For more information, please contact the publisher.

Cider Mill Press Book Publishers
"Where Good Books Are Ready for Press"
PO Box 454
12 Spring Street
Kennebunkport, Maine 04046
Visit us online! www.cidermillpress.com

Typography: Bushcraft, Fenwick Park JF, Helvetica Rounded, Neutraface 2 Text, Sentinel, Hello Beautiful
Image Credits on page 239.

Printed in China
1 2 3 4 5 6 7 8 9 0
First Edition

PIZZAS

and FLATBREADS

OVER 100 RECIPES FEATURING EVERYONE'S FAVORITE COMFORT FOODS

CIDER MILL
PRESS

BOOK
PUBLISHERS

KENNEBUNKPORT, MAINE

Contents

Introduction

If you polled Westerners on the one food they'd refuse to give up, it seems assured that pizza would claim the top spot. Simple, affordable, versatile, and—most importantly—delicious, this doughy delight has risen from its humble origins (it was initially consumed by poor Neapolitans) to win the hearts and taste buds of people the world over.

That said, the universal love has allowed some pretty mediocre shops to take root in our communities. Relying on people's at-times-insatiable need for a fix, a number of places are happy to do the bare minimum and put out a product that scratches the itch but comes nowhere near the level we know to be available.

But there's good news: great pizza is easy to make at home. *Pizzas and Flatbreads* will walk you through each step of the process, giving you control over the dough, sauce, toppings, and texture and taking your precious pie out of the hands of the indifferent. Since this cookbook provides the basics as well as a few recipes that will get you thinking outside of the box, your days of lackluster pizza are soon to be a thing of the past.

While pizza is clearly king, it is in no way the only flatbread with authority. Flatbreads have established themselves as the cornerstones of cuisines all over the globe, whether it be the tortilla from Mexico or the Greek pita. As versatile as their Italian cousin, they provide a solid foundation for numerous classics and exciting innovations.

With dough recipes as well as inventive ideas for sauces and toppings that will keep you from getting stuck in a rut, *Pizzas and Flatbreads* is here to ensure that each of your interactions with these beloved comfort foods is nothing short of remarkable.

Tips & Techniques

While making your own pizzas and flatbreads isn't difficult, there are a few things you'll want to have squared away before you start serving up your creations. Since baking is largely chemistry, even slight variations can have a large effect on the end product.

For instance, is your tap water basic, neutral, or acidic? This small detail is irrelevant for most preparations, but will have a large effect on the flavor and texture of your dough. Proper kneading and shaping are also crucial to producing pizzas and flatbreads that are up to snuff, and we've got everything you need to take these important matters into your own hands.

IT'S IN THE WATER

You may have heard claims that a certain bread or food cannot be made in any place other than the place where it originated, because the real secret for the recipe's success is "in the water." It is often claimed that an authentic Neapolitan pizza can only be made in Naples, because of the water, or that pizza outside New York City suffers because of differences in what's coming from the tap. And while this may be an exaggeration, there are two main qualities that should be considered when making pizzas and flatbreads, the hardness and pH of the water.

Water Hardness

The hardness of water depends on the concentration of mineral salts, especially calcium and magnesium. These minerals interact with proteins, affecting the dough development in different ways. Specifically, a very soft water (up to 5 mg/L) can collapse a dough, while too hard of a water (over 120 mg/L) results in poor production of gases, reduces the activity of the yeasts, and creates a tighter gluten net, which results in a forced extension of leavening times. Information on water hardness is often made available by local municipalities. If you plan to use your tap water, you will want to check this information and evaluate if you need to dilute your water with bottled water to reach the right balance of minerals. Water

filters may also come in handy if your water is too hard.

Water pH

A neutral solution has a pH of 7, a basic pH is greater than 7, and an acidic solution has a pH less than 7. For bread dough, it is generally preferable to use a slightly acidic water with a pH around 5 or 6, but Neapolitan dough likes a neutral pH. If your tap water is basic, consider diluting it with bottled water to lower the pH.

MAKING PIZZA AT HOME

If you have never made pizza, it is best to start with an easy–to–prepare dough such as the Basic Pizza Dough on page 17 and then move from there.

Kneading the Dough

If you own a standing mixer: Put the dough hook on and knead at a low speed for 5 minutes. Then, increase to medium speed and work the dough for 5 more minutes. Check the dough by picking up a piece of it: Is it crumbly? If so, knead at a low speed for 3 minutes and increase the speed to medium–high for 2 minutes. If the piece of dough elongates elastically without detaching completely from the rest of dough as you pull it away, then your dough is ready.

By hand: Work the dough on a solid surface and let it rest every few minutes. This helps the gluten net form on its own and gives the dough time to relax. Keep working the dough at regular intervals, covering it in between the intervals, until it feels smooth and elastic when you pull at one corner. Do not worry too much about your technique. Hand kneading is a very intuitive process: let your hands do the job and learn to feel the dough. It is also a wonderful way to relieve stress, so enjoy.

First Fermentation

When the dough feels smooth and elastic, form it into a ball and place it in an airtight container or in a bowl covered with plastic wrap, making sure that the dough has enough space to triple in size (though it may not need to). Depending on room temperature, the dough will take between 1½ to 2 hours to double in volume.

Second Fermentation

This is where having a scale comes in handy. Transfer your dough to a clean working surface, divide it into ½ pound pieces, and form them into rounds. Place them in a heavily floured pan, leaving enough space between them so that they can rise. Sprinkle the rounds with flour and cover them with a kitchen towel. Make sure they do not dry out, or it will be difficult to flatten them later. The second fermentation should allow the rounds to increase their volume by 50 percent. Do not let them sit too long, because the dough will soften too much and become difficult to shape.

Shaping the Pizza

This may be the hardest part of making quality pizza. However, you will become better and better as time goes by. As a rule of thumb, you want to avoid using a rolling pin on your pizza if possible. To do this, place the ball of dough on a well–floured surface. Press your fingers firmly into the center of the ball and work out toward the edge, opening the dough little by little. Make sure to leave a ½–inch border at the edge of the dough. Turn the dough over, repeat the pressing–out process, and then place the flattened dough on the back of your hands, ensuring that the weight is on your knuckles. Turn the dough 90° at a time until the tension in the dough is gone. The dough is ready when it is loose, thin, and approximately 10 inches in diameter.

Cooking the Pizza

Standard Kitchen Oven: You probably don't have the resources or the time to have a wood–fired pizza oven at your house, but don't worry—your regular old oven will work just fine. Heat is the most important element for making a good pizza crust, so you will want to have your oven set to its maximum temperature when cooking a pizza. A baking stone will also help you get consistently great results. To use the stone, place it in the oven as the oven heats up so that the stone gets really hot. Once you are ready to cook the pizza, dust the stone with cornmeal and use a peel (or the back of a greased nonstick pizza pan) to transfer the dough onto the stone.

Generally, the stone is placed on the middle rack of the oven, but you can also place the stone on a higher rack, which will result in shorter cooking time and a softer crust. If you don't have a baking stone, a nonstick pizza pan will also work.

Grill: A gas or charcoal grill is capable of producing fantastic pizza that has a charred, wood–fired touch. If you are going to make pizza on the grill, a baking stone that is suitable for a grill is a must. Seek out a lighter, round stone that can handle high temperatures. A lid for the grill is also essential, as it will keep the steam from the dough in and allow the pizza to cook properly and at a high temperature.

Pizza Doughs

Don't listen to anyone who suggests otherwise: the key to great pizza is the dough. With that in mind, we provide you with a series of easy, flavorful doughs that will provide an ideal foundation upon which to build your next pizza party.

Whether it is the classic Neapolitan Pizza Dough (see page 18) or the peerless Gluten–Free Pizza Dough (see page 25), we help you take the first step to moving beyond the overpriced, mediocre shop down the street.

Basic Pizza Dough

**YIELD: 8 BALLS OF DOUGH • ACTIVE TIME: 30 MINUTES
TOTAL TIME: 2½ HOURS**

This is the perfect dough to start out with, as it will produce delicious pizzas and help you develop your feel for other, more delicate doughs.

1 Combine all of the dry ingredients and create a well in the center. Carefully pour the water into the well and gradually incorporate it into the flour mixture. It will take 3 to 4 minutes for the dough to come together. If the dough is too dry, add water in 1–tablespoon increments until the dough holds together.

2 Knead the dough until it is smooth and springy, yet soft. This should take about 10 minutes. It should be possible to stretch the dough so thin that it is translucent when held up to the light. Place the dough in a large bowl, cover with a tea towel, and store in a naturally warm spot for 1½ to 2 hours.

3 After the dough has doubled in size, divide it into eight even–sized balls and place them under a tea towel for 10 to 15 minutes.

4 If using, stretch the balls of dough into 10–inch rounds. If not using immediately, place in plastic bags and store in the freezer for up to 2 weeks.

INGREDIENTS

7½ cups high–protein baker's flour

2 tablespoons dry yeast, plus 1 teaspooon

2¾ teaspoons salt

2½ cups cold water (about 60°F), plus more as needed

Neapolitan Pizza Dough

YIELD: 10 BALLS OF DOUGH • ACTIVE TIME: 25 MINUTES
TOTAL TIME: 8½ TO 24 HOURS

This dough is a large part of the reason that pizza has become beloved all over the world, and it's well worth the time and effort necessary to get it right.

INGREDIENTS

8 cups high–gluten flour

⅔ teaspoon fresh baker's yeast

2½ cups cold water (about 60°F)

3½ teaspoons salt

1 Place the flour on your work surface and make a well in the center. Dissolve the yeast in the water and then pour this mixture into the middle of the well a little at a time while using your hands to incorporate the flour. Once the mixture achieves the consistency of custard, add the salt and incorporate the rest of the flour until the mixture holds together as a dough. Knead for 10 to 15 minutes until the dough is smooth and elastic. Cover and let stand for 10 minutes, and then knead again for 10 seconds, which helps develop the flavor and the gluten.

2 Divide the dough into 10 even–sized balls, place them in deep baking dishes, sprinkle them with flour, cover with tea towels, and let stand for at least 8 hours, and up to 24 hours.

3 If using, stretch the balls of dough into 10–inch rounds. If not using immediately, place each of them in a plastic bag and freeze for up to 2 weeks.

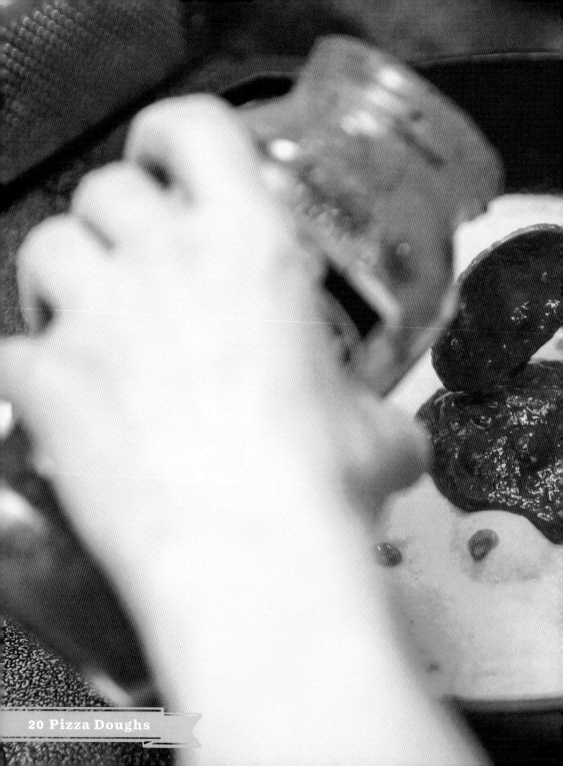

Skillet Pizza Dough

YIELD: 2 BALLS OF DOUGH • ACTIVE TIME: 25 MINUTES
TOTAL TIME: ABOUT 2½ HOURS

A cast–iron skillet is a great tool for cooking pizza, as it's famous ability to evenly distribute heat results in a crisp yet chewy crust.

1 Using a standing mixer with a dough hook, place the water, butter, and olive oil into the mixing bowl. Then add half of the flour, half of the semolina, the yeast, salt, and sugar and mix for 3 to 4 minutes until the mixture is a nice, smooth batter. Cover the bowl with a tea towel or plastic wrap and let rest for 20 minutes.

2 Add the remaining flour and semolina and mix on low speed for 7 minutes. The dough will be soft and tacky, and look more like a batter.

3 Take the slightly yellow dough and divide it into two sections. Mold the pieces of dough into smooth balls and rub each with the remaining olive oil. Place them each in a large bowl, cover with tea towels, and let them rest for 1 hour.

4 Place a ball of dough in the skillet and spread evenly around, getting it to about 1 inch from the top as you push it up the edge. Once you have done that, cover the pan with a tea towel and let the dough rest for 30 minutes before cooking. If not using immediately, place each of the balls of dough in a plastic bag and freeze for up to 2 weeks.

INGREDIENTS

1¾ cups water

3 tablespoons butter

¾ cup olive oil, plus 1 tablespoon

4¾ cups all–purpose flour

½ cup fine semolina flour

2 tablespoons dry yeast, plus 1 teaspoon

1 teaspoon salt

1 teaspoon sugar

Whole Wheat Pizza Dough

**YIELD: 1 BALL OF DOUGH • ACTIVE TIME: 15 MINUTES
TOTAL TIME: 30 MINUTES**

Because pizza dough needs to be elastic, it's best to keep some all–purpose flour in the mix. The honey helps activate the yeast, and mellows the whole wheat flavor just enough.

INGREDIENTS

¾ cup warm water (110°F)

½ teaspoon honey

1 teaspoon active dry yeast

1½ cups wheat flour

½ cup all–purpose flour, plus more as needed

1½ teaspoons salt

1 In a large bowl, add the water, honey, and yeast and stir until the yeast dissolves. Stir in the flours and salt and mix until the dough is just combined. It will be sticky.

2 Turn the dough out on a floured surface and start kneading until the flour is incorporated. If necessary, add more flour until the dough is elastic and smooth. Allow the dough to rest for 15 minutes.

3 If using, stretch the ball of dough into a 9–inch round. If not using immediately, place in a plastic bag and freeze for up to 2 weeks.

Gluten–Free Pizza Dough

YIELD: 2 BALLS OF DOUGH • ACTIVE TIME: 15 MINUTES
TOTAL TIME: 15 MINUTES

Pizza can be tough for the gluten intolerant, but the dog days are over. With this simple, delicious dough, you might even convert the most steadfast gluten devotee.

1 Combine the yeast and ³/₄ cup of the water in a small bowl and let stand. After 2 or 3 minutes, stir in 1 tablespoon of the sugar and let stand for another couple of minutes.

2 In a separate bowl, combine the flours. Add the xanthan gum, salt, baking powder, and the remaining sugar. Whisk until well combined.

3 Make a well in the dry mixture and then add the yeast mixture. Add the olive oil and the remaining water. Using a wooden spoon, stir until well combined. This dough is best if used immediately, but it will keep in the refrigerator for 1 to 2 days.

INGREDIENTS

1 tablespoon yeast

1¼ cups warm water (110°F)

3 tablespoons sugar

1 cup white rice flour

1 cup brown rice flour

1 cup tapioca flour

¾ teaspoon xanthan gum

1 teaspoon salt

½ teaspoon baking powder

1 tablespoon olive oil

Paleo Pizza Dough

**YIELD: 1 BALL OF DOUGH • ACTIVE TIME: 30 MINUTES
TOTAL TIME: 30 MINUTES**

A huge benefit of trends like the Paleo Diet is that they have opened people's eyes to the incredible versatility of cauliflower, which is much more than its bland appearance suggests.

INGREDIENTS

1 head of cauliflower, cut into florets

2 eggs, lightly beaten

1 tablespoon Italian seasoning

Salt and pepper, to taste

1 Place the cauliflower in a food processor and pulse until it has a rice–like consistency.

2 Fill a large pot about ⅓ full of water, bring to a boil, and place the cauliflower in it. Cook until soft, about 5 minutes, drain, and transfer to a clean dish towel. Squeeze out as much water as possible and then place the cauliflower in a large mixing bowl.

3 Add the eggs to the bowl, season with the Italian seasoning, salt, and pepper, and stir until well combined.

4 Place the mixture on a piece of parchment paper and shape into a 10–inch crust. Use a spatula to carefully transfer the crust to a pizza pan or cast–iron skillet. Add desired toppings and cook in a 450°F oven.

Pizzas with Meat

For some, pizza is little more than a vehicle for delicious, salty meats. And yes, it is easy to just pile a bunch of pepperoni or sausage on a pizza and get a delicious result.

But there's no reason to limit yourself. For those individuals who want a little more from their pizzas but are struggling to see beyond the standards, we've gathered a few inventive offerings—such as the Mashed Potato, Bacon, and Scallion Pizza on page 42—that are sure to electrify both mind and mouth.

Salami and Broccoli Pizza

YIELD: 1 PIZZA • ACTIVE TIME: 15 MINUTES
TOTAL TIME: 25 MINUTES

Everyone knows and loves Italian sausage on pizza. Here, we've spiced things up with hard salami and added some broccoli to create a whirlwind of flavor.

1 Preheat your oven to 550°F. Wash the broccoli and boil in salted water for 3 minutes. Drain and cut into big chunks.

2 Place the broccoli, 1 tablespoon olive oil, and the garlic in a frying pan and sauté for 3 minutes.

3 Spread 1 tablespoon of olive oil over the pizza dough. Distribute the mozzarella over the pizza and place the broccoli on top. Top with the salami, season with salt and pepper, and sprinkle with the pecorino. Drizzle with the remaining olive oil and cook until the crust is golden brown and the cheese is browned and bubbly.

INGREDIENTS

½ cup broccoli

3 tablespoons olive oil

1 garlic clove, minced

1 ball of dough, stretched into a 10-inch round

¾ cup fresh mozzarella, drained and sliced

⅔ cup hard salami, chopped

Salt and black pepper, to taste

1 tablespoon pecorino Romano cheese, grated

Parma Ham and Smoked Cheese Pizza

YIELD: 1 PIZZA • ACTIVE TIME: 15 MINUTES
TOTAL TIME: 25 MINUTES

This pizza is reminiscent of something you might find in a small Roman café. This recipe relies on the quality of the ham and cheeses, so be sure not to skimp.

INGREDIENTS

2 tablespoons olive oil

1 ball of dough, stretched into a 10–inch round

¾ cup fresh mozzarella, drained and sliced

¾ cup smoked cheese (such as provola), sliced

Salt and black pepper, to taste

3 slices of Parma ham, chopped

1 tablespoon Parmesan cheese, grated

1 Preheat your oven to 550°F. Pour and distribute 1 tablespoon of olive oil over the pizza dough. Distribute the mozzarella over the pizza.

2 Distribute the smoked cheese over the mozzarella. Season with salt and pepper, top with the ham and Parmesan, and drizzle with the remaining olive oil. Cook until the crust is golden brown and the cheese is browned and bubbly.

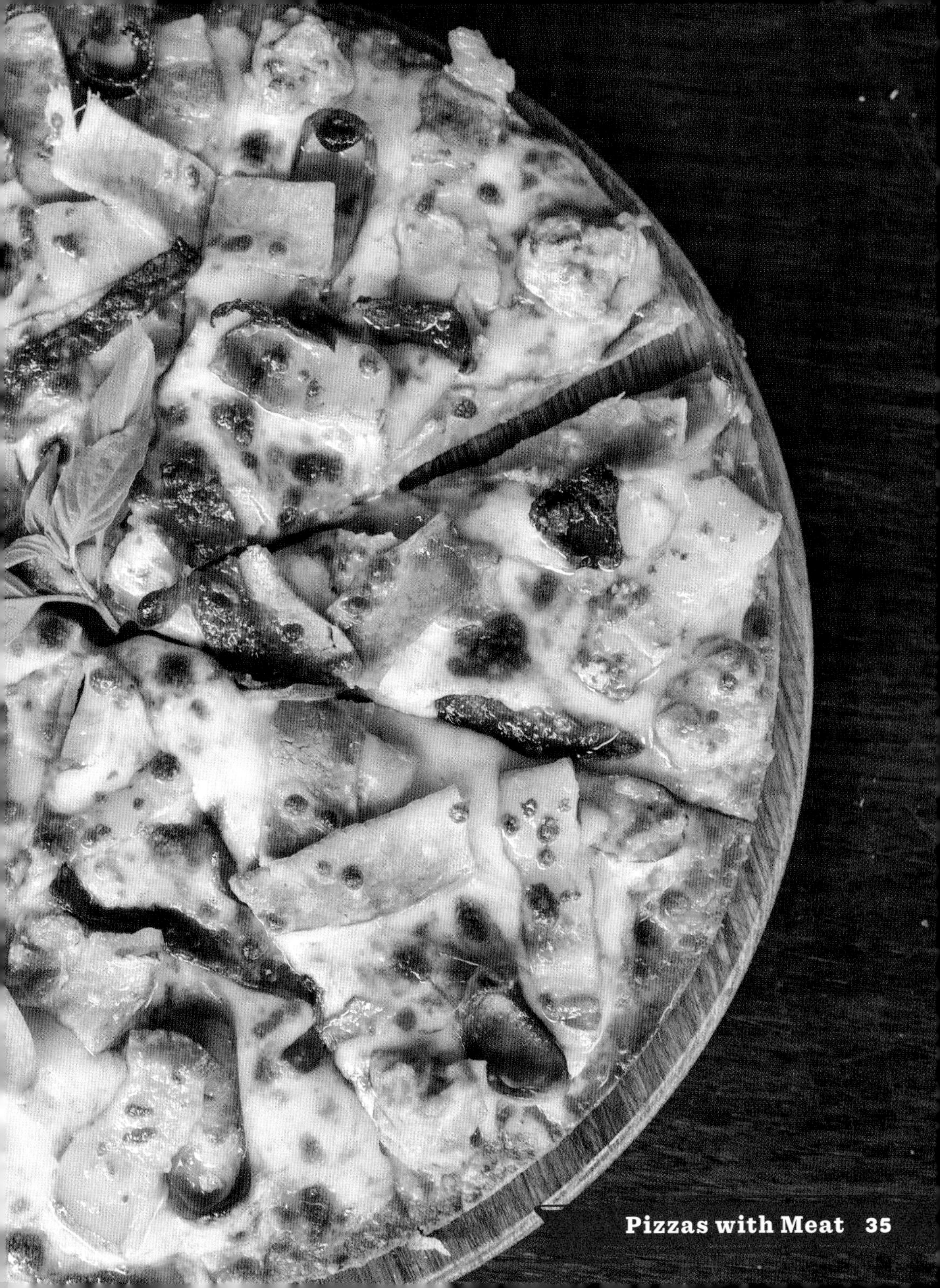

Chorizo and Olive Pizza

YIELD: 1 PIZZA • ACTIVE TIME: 20 MINUTES
TOTAL TIME: 30 MINUTES

If you're in the mood for something savory, the combination of chorizo and olives is tough to beat.

1 Preheat your oven to 550°F. Spread the tomato sauce over the pizza dough and then distribute the mozzarella over the sauce.

2 Distribute the chorizo slices and olives over the mozzarella. Sprinkle with the Parmesan, season with salt and pepper, and drizzle with the olive oil. Cook until the crust is golden brown and the cheese is browned and bubbly.

Variation: If you like the idea of chorizo on a pizza but aren't a fan of olives, use slices of red bell pepper instead.

INGREDIENTS

⅓ cup tomato sauce, homemade (see page), canned or fresh

1 ball of dough, stretched into a 10-inch round

¾ cup fresh mozzarella, drained and sliced

½ cup chorizo, sliced

½ cup black olives, pitted and chopped

1 tablespoon Parmesan cheese, grated

Salt and black pepper, to taste

1 tablespoon olive oil

Deep Dish Bacon Pizza

YIELD: 1 PIZZA • ACTIVE TIME: 45 MINUTES
TOTAL TIME: 1 HOUR

Break out the cast–iron skillet and loosen your belt, because this deep dish is both decadent and irresistible.

INGREDIENTS

1 ball of Skillet Pizza Dough (see page 21), stretched to 12 inches

1½ cups mozzarella, grated

½ cup bacon, roughly chopped

1 tablespoon Parmesan cheese, grated

2 tablespoons Bacon Jam (see page 41)

Maple syrup, for serving

1 Preheat your oven to 550°F. Working with the dough in the skillet, sprinkle half of the mozzarella over the dough.

2 Distribute ¼ cup of the bacon on top of the cheese and top with the rest of the mozzarella.

3 Top with the remaining bacon and sprinkle with the Parmesan. Distribute small dollops of the Bacon Jam evenly over the pizza and place it in the oven.

4 Cook until the crust is golden brown and the cheese is browned and bubbly, about 10 minutes. Remove the pizza from the oven and let it sit for 5 minutes. Serve with maple syrup on the side.

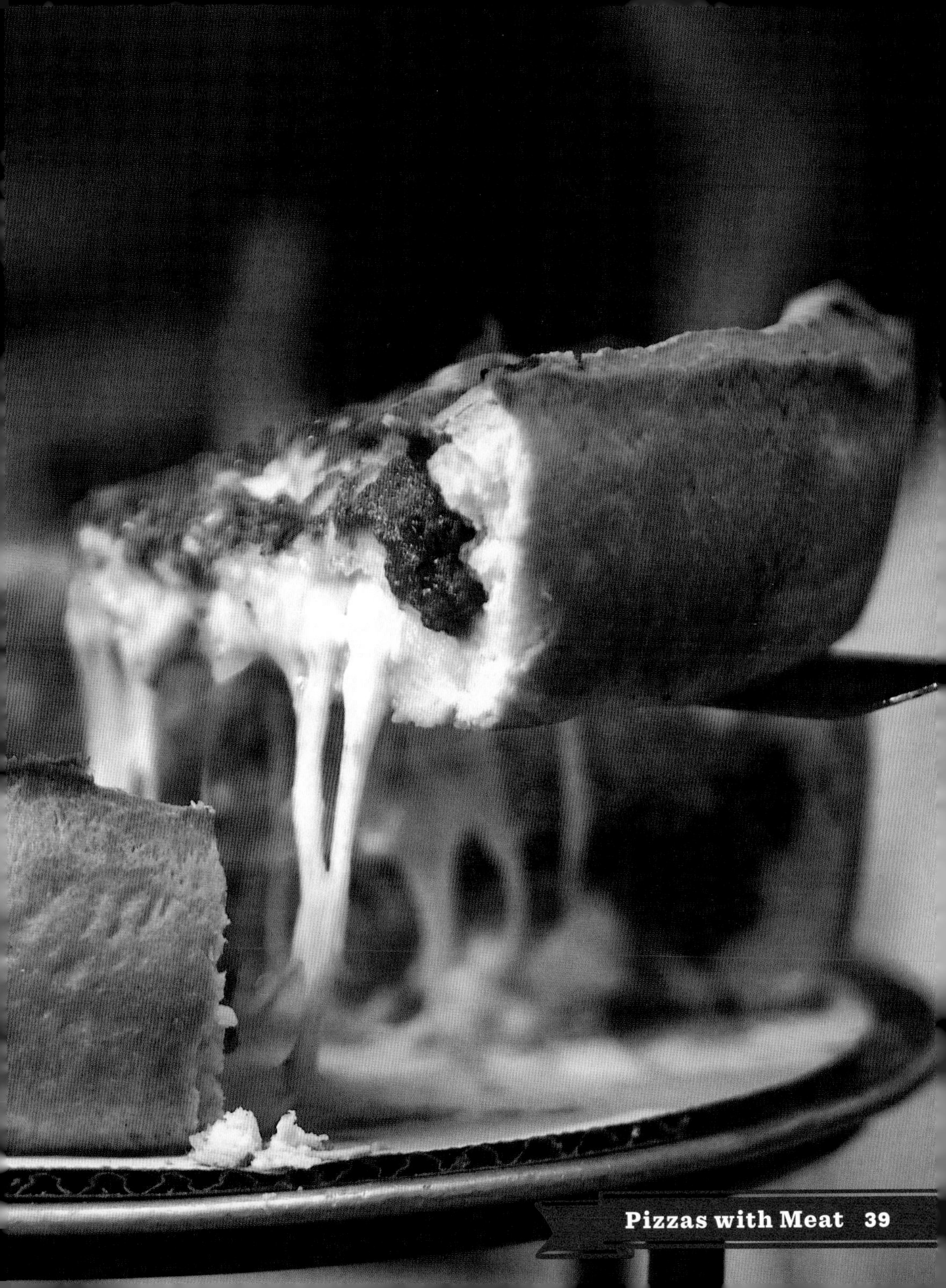

Bacon Jam

Salty, smoky bacon in a sweet, spreadable form is almost too good to be believed.

1 Place the oil, bacon, tomatoes, and onions in a medium saucepan and cook over medium–high heat for 10 minutes, while stirring occasionally.

2 Add the stock, sugar, molasses, water, and cayenne pepper and cook for 30 minutes, while stirring occasionally.

3 Remove the pan from the stove and let cool. When cool, store in the refrigerator for 2 to 3 weeks.

Tip: File this recipe away, as this bacon jam is a wonderful spread for any of the flatbreads in this book, as well as crackers and crostini.

INGREDIENTS

1 tablespoon vegetable oil

1 cup bacon, chopped

1 cup cherry tomatoes, thinly sliced

1 cup red onion, minced

1 cup chicken stock

1 cup sugar

4 tablespoons molasses

1 cup water

½ teaspoon cayenne pepper

Mashed Potato, Bacon, and Scallion Pizza

YIELD: 1 PIZZA • ACTIVE TIME: 25 MINUTES
TOTAL TIME: 45 MINUTES

This funky recipe comes courtesy of OTTO, the great New England pizzeria chain. Try it and you'll see why they always seem to be opening a new location.

INGREDIENTS

1 ball of dough, stretched into a 10-inch round

2 tablespoons olive oil

Salt and black pepper, to taste

2 tablespoons Asiago cheese, grated

¾ cup mashed potatoes

1½ cups mozzarella, grated

Heavy cream, to taste

½ cup bacon, cooked and chopped

½ cup scallions, chopped

1 tablespoon of parsley, rosemary, and thyme mixture

1 Preheat your oven to 550°F. Brush the dough with olive oil. Season with pepper and sprinkle the Asiago over the dough. Spread the mashed potatoes over the dough and then top with the mozzarella.

2 Drizzle generously with the cream and top with the bacon, scallions, and herb mixture. Season with salt and place in the oven. Cook, while rotating the pizza halfway through, until golden brown, about 15 to 20 minutes.

White Pizza with Fennel Sausage

YIELD: 1 PIZZA • ACTIVE TIME: 25 MINUTES
TOTAL TIME: 35 MINUTES

This savory pizza is so tasty that it's worth the extra heaviness provided by the potato.

1 Preheat your oven to 550°F. Distribute the smoked mozzarella, sausage, potato, and onion over the pizza dough. Sprinkle the rosemary and salt on top, drizzle with the olive oil, and place in the oven.

2 Cook until the crust is golden brown and the cheese is browned and bubbly, about 10 minutes. Remove from the oven and garnish with additional rosemary before serving.

INGREDIENTS

¾ to 1 cup smoked mozzarella, cut into thin cubes

1 fennel sausage, cut into pieces and cooked

½ baked potato, chopped

¼ red onion, sliced thin

1 ball of pizza dough, stretched into a 10-inch round

Leaves from 2 sprigs of rosemary, plus more for garnish

Pinch of salt

1 tablespoon olive oil

Roast Beef and Spinach Pizza

YIELD: 1 PIZZA • ACTIVE TIME: 15 MINUTES
TOTAL TIME: 25 MINUTES

A classic combo, this pie will keep you singing its praises for days. The spinach and mozzarella pair perfectly together, and the roast beef tops off the concoction.

INGREDIENTS

1 handful of spinach

3 tablespoons olive oil

1 ball of pizza dough, stretched into a 10-inch round

¾ cup fresh mozzarella, drained and sliced

¾ cup thinly sliced roast beef, cut into strips

Salt and black pepper, to taste

1 Preheat the oven to 550°F. Place the spinach in a bowl and toss with 1 tablespoon of the olive oil. Pour and distribute another tablespoon of the olive oil over the pizza dough.

2 Distribute the mozzarella over the pizza. Top with the spinach and then distribute the roast beef evenly over the pizza. Drizzle with the remaining olive oil and season with salt and pepper.

3 Cook until the crust is golden brown and the cheese is browned and bubbly, about 10 minutes.

Tip: If you have time to prepare some hollandaise sauce, it makes for a lovely accompaniment. Just drizzle 2 tablespoons over the pizza before placing it in the oven.

Shrimp, Pink Mayonnaise, and Lettuce Pizza

YIELD: 1 PIZZA • ACTIVE TIME: 15 MINUTES
TOTAL TIME: 35 MINUTES

This recipe may look strange to some, but your taste buds don't have eyeballs. It's delicious, and a great way to use up leftover shrimp.

1 Preheat the oven to 550°F. Spread the tomato sauce over the pizza dough. Drizzle with 1 tablespoon of the olive oil, season with salt and pepper, and cook until the crust is golden brown, about 10 minutes.

2 Let the pizza cool and then spread the Pink Mayonnaise over the tomato sauce. Distribute the shrimp and the lettuce over the top and season with salt and pepper. Drizzle with the remaining olive oil and serve.

Tip: Pink mayonnaise is extremely easy to make. Simply combine ½ cup mayonnaise, ¼ cup ketchup, and ¼ teaspoon lime juice in a small bowl, season with salt and pepper, and refrigerate until ready to use.

INGREDIENTS

⅓ cup tomato sauce, homemade (see page 129) or store-bought

1 ball of pizza dough, stretched into a 10-inch round

2 tablespoons olive oil

Salt and black pepper, to taste

2 tablespoons pink mayonnaise (see tip)

½ cup shrimp, deveined, cooked, and peeled

1 handful of lettuce, chopped

Anchovies and Mozzarella Pizza

Anchovies on pizza have historically gotten a bad rap, to the point that it was a running joke in the early '90s. Luckily, increased appreciation for umami has rehabbed that image.

INGREDIENTS

⅓ cup tomato sauce, homemade (see page 129) or store-bought

1 ball of dough, stretched into a 10-inch round

¾ cup fresh mozzarella, drained and sliced

5 to 6 anchovy fillets, halved

Salt, to taste

Oregano, to taste

1 tablespoon Parmesan cheese, grated

1 teaspoon olive oil

1 Preheat the oven to 550°F. Spread the tomato sauce over the pizza dough. Distribute the mozzarella over the sauce and top with the anchovies.

2 Distribute the pieces of anchovy evenly over the mozzarella. Season with salt and oregano and sprinkle the Parmesan on top. Drizzle with the olive oil and cook until the crust is golden brown and the cheese is bubbly, about 10 minutes.

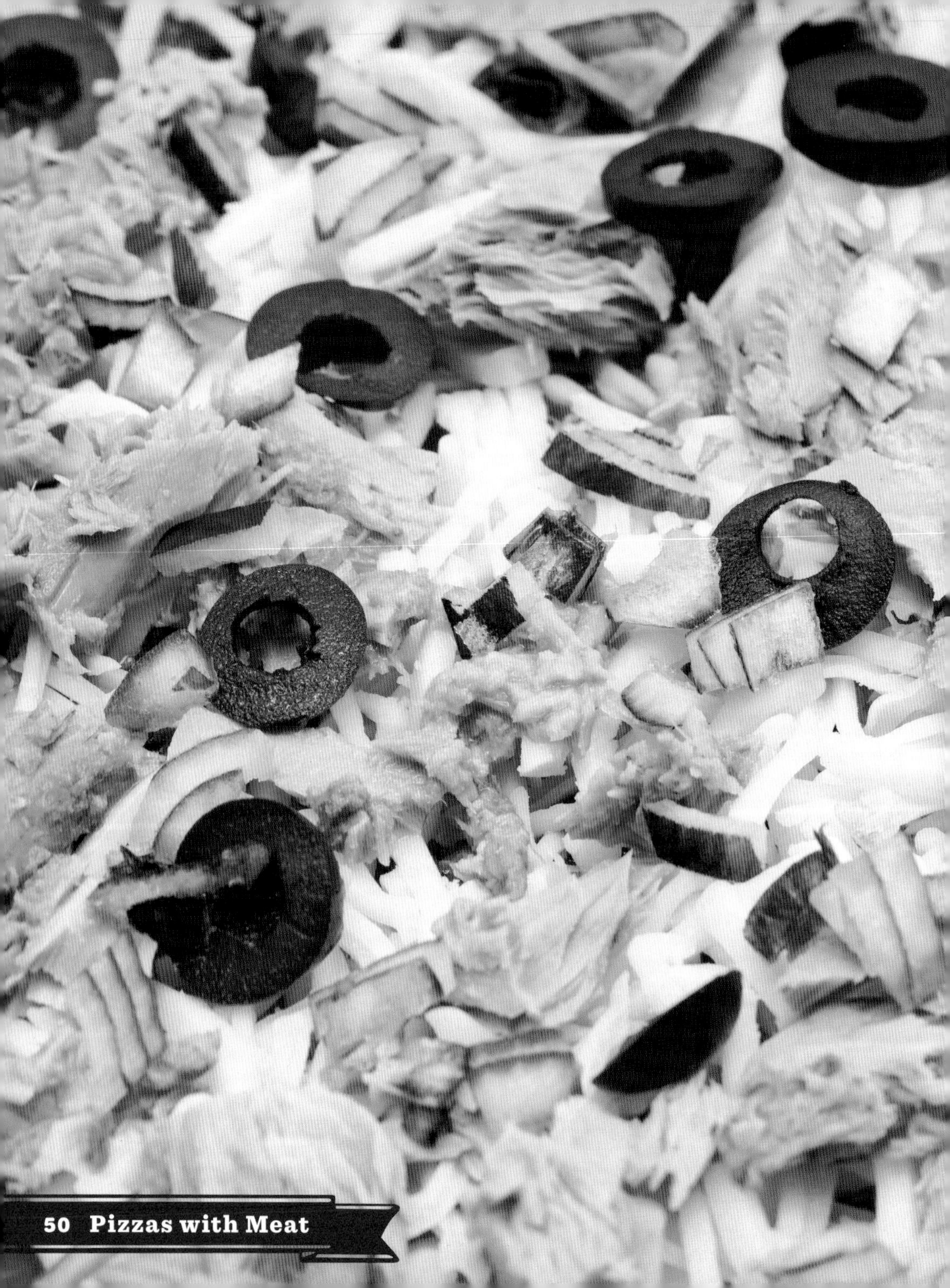

Tuna Fish, Red Onion, and Black Olive Pizza

YIELD: 1 PIZZA • ACTIVE TIME: 15 MINUTES
TOTAL TIME: 35 MINUTES

This pizza tastes like it came straight from southern Italy, where it is common to make use of the abundance of fantastic fish. This pizza is great as an appetizer, but if you toss a small salad beside it, it can easily serve as a main course.

1 Preheat the oven to 550°F. Spread the tomato sauce over the pizza dough. Distribute the mozzarella over the sauce and top with the tuna. Distribute the onion slices and olives on top.

2 Season with salt and pepper, drizzle with the olive oil, and cook until the crust is golden brown and the cheese is bubbly, about 10 minutes.

INGREDIENTS

⅓ cup tomato sauce, homemade (see page 129) or store–bought

1 ball of dough, stretched into a 10–inch round

¾ cup fresh mozzarella, drained and sliced

⅔ cup canned tuna fish in olive oil, drained

¼ red onion, sliced thin

1 handful of black olives, pitted

Salt and black pepper, to taste

1 tablespoon olive oil

Smoked Salmon and Spinach Pizza

YIELD: 1 PIZZA • ACTIVE TIME: 15 MINUTES
TOTAL TIME: 35 MINUTES

Salty and loaded with omega-3s, smoked salmon is a healthy topping that doesn't sacrifice any flavor.

INGREDIENTS

1 handful of spinach

3 tablespoons olive oil

1 ball of dough, stretched into a 10–inch round

¾ cup fresh mozzarella, drained and sliced

⅓ cup smoked salmon, sliced thin

Salt and black pepper, to taste

1 Preheat the oven to 550°F. Place the spinach in a bowl and toss with 1 tablespoon of the olive oil. Pour and distribute another tablespoon of olive oil over the pizza dough.

2 Distribute the mozzarella over the dough and top with the spinach. Distribute the smoked salmon over the spinach, season with salt and pepper, and drizzle with the remaining olive oil.

3 Place in the oven and cook until the crust is golden brown and the cheese is bubbly, about 10 minutes.

Variation: If you're looking for something to counter the savory salmon, spread tomato sauce on the dough before adding the mozzarella. You can also add some salmon roe and shrimp after you remove the pizza from the oven.

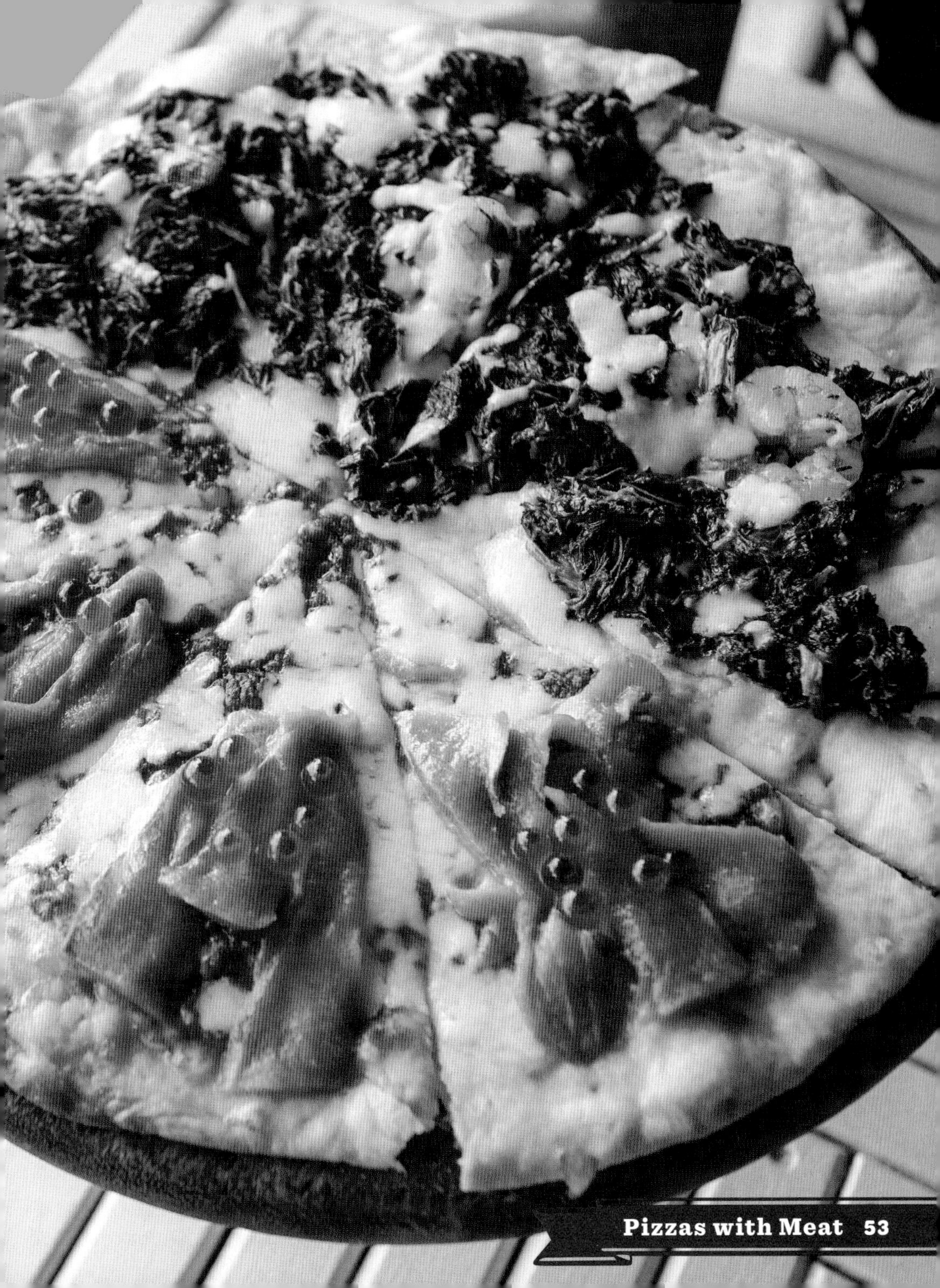

Salt & Pepper Prawn Pizza

YIELD: 1 PIZZA • ACTIVE TIME: 25 MINUTES
TOTAL TIME: 45 MINUTES

As beautiful as this pizza looks and as wonderful as it tastes, it is incredibly simple to prepare. In other words, it captures everything that is great about pizza.

INGREDIENTS

For the Sriracha Mayo
1 cup Sriracha sauce
1 cup mayonnaise
Juice of 1 lemon
Pinch of salt

For the Avocado Mousse
Meat from 2 avocados
Pinch of salt
Juice of 1 lemon

For the Pizza
1 cup arugula
1 tablespoon olive oil
Pinch of salt

1 teaspoon sesame seeds, plus more for garnish
Pinch of pepper
10 large raw prawns, shelled and deveined
1 teaspoon garlic, minced
1 ball of dough, stretched into a 10-inch round
¾ to 1 cup mozzarella, grated

1 Preheat the oven to 430°F. Combine all of the ingredients for the Sriracha Mayo in a small bowl and whisk until combined. Cover and set aside.

2 Combine all of the ingredients for the Avocado Mousse in a small bowl and whisk until combined. Cover and set aside.

3 Place the arugula in a bowl and toss with the olive oil. Combine the salt, sesame seeds, and pepper in a small bowl, add the prawns, and toss to coat. Set both bowls aside.

4 Sprinkle the garlic over the pizza dough and then distribute the mozzarella.

5 Distribute the prawns evenly over the pizza. Place in the oven and bake for 7 to 10 minutes, until the crust is golden brown and the cheese is bubbly.

6 Remove the pizza from the oven, top it with the arugula and drizzle with the Sriracha Mayo. Distribute dollops of Avocado Mousse evenly around pizza and sprinkle with the additional sesame seeds before serving.

Vegetarian Pizzas

Sometimes you find yourself with a fridge full of vegetables and no way to employ them all. Sometimes you don't want the glorious trinity of dough, sauce, and cheese to be drowned out by the rich flavor of meat. Sometimes you just want to bask in the fresh flavor of veggies.

If you find yourself in any of these camps, we've got an array of delicious vegetarian options that lack the heft of their meat–based brethren but none of the flavor. We are particularly fond of the sweet yet earthy Bok Choy, Pine Nut, and Raisin Pizza (see page 73) and the zesty Tomato and Goat Cheese Pizza (see page 79).

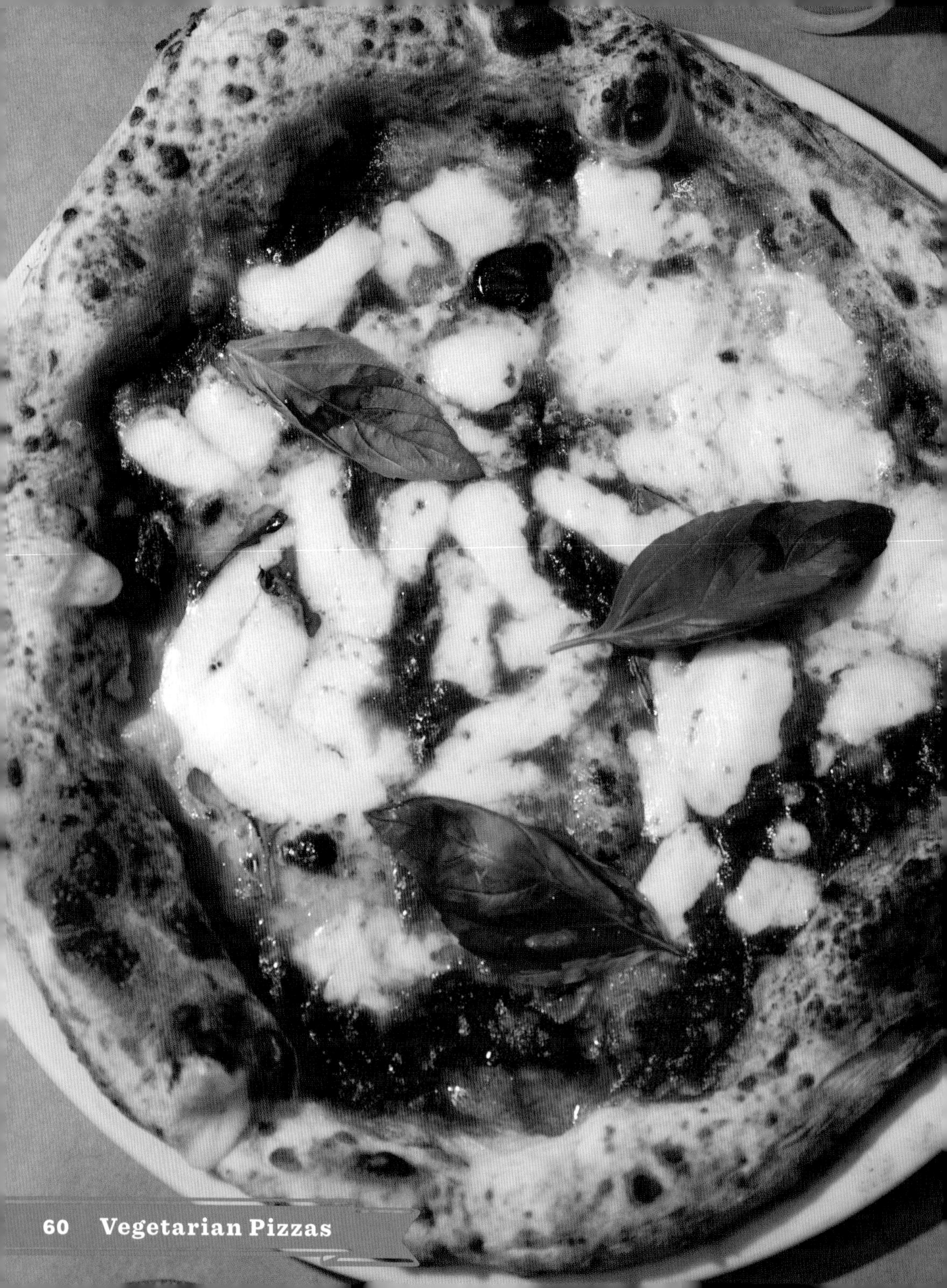

The Margherita

YIELD: 1 PIZZA • ACTIVE TIME: 20 MINUTES
TOTAL TIME: 30 MINUTES

Simple, delicious, and economical. This is the pizza that launched the global revolution.

1 Preheat the oven to 550°F. Spread the tomato sauce over the pizza dough. Distribute the mozzarella over the sauce and then sprinkle the Parmesan on top.

2 Distribute the basil leaves over the pizza. Season with salt, place in the oven, and cook until the crust is golden brown and the cheese is bubbly. Remove from the oven, drizzle with olive oil, and serve.

INGREDIENTS

⅓ cup tomato sauce, homemade (see page 129) or store-bought

1 ball of pizza dough, stretched into a 10-inch round

¾ cup fresh mozzarella, drained and sliced

1 tablespoon Parmesan cheese, grated

6 to 8 basil leaves

Salt, to taste

1 teaspoon olive oil

Grilled White Pizza with Peppers

YIELD: 1 PIZZA • ACTIVE TIME: 10 MINUTES
TOTAL TIME: 25 MINUTES

The bit of char added by the grill goes a long way on this flavorful pizza.

INGREDIENTS

1 tablespoon olive oil, plus more for brushing

1 ball of dough, stretched into a 10-inch round

1 cup bell peppers, cut into strips

1 garlic clove, minced

1 cup mozzarella, grated

¼ red onion, sliced

2 tablespoons goat cheese, crumbled

2 tablespoons Parmesan cheese

2 basil leaves, torn

Salt and pepper, to taste

1 Preheat your gas or charcoal grill to high heat and brush the surface with olive oil.

2 When the grill is 500°F, place the dough on the grill and cook with the lid closed for about 2 minutes, or until it becomes slightly browned. Flip over and grill for another 2 minutes. Make sure the dough is golden brown and has slight grill marks. Remove from heat and set aside.

3 Brush the tablespoon of olive oil over the bell pepper strips and grill for about 4 minutes, turning the slices over halfway through. Lightly brush olive oil over the cooked dough and sprinkle the garlic on top. Evenly distribute the mozzarella, cooked bell peppers, onion, and goat cheese over the pizza.

4 Place the pizza back on the grill and cook until the cheeses have melted. Remove from heat and top with the Parmesan and basil. Season with salt and pepper and serve.

Wild Mushroom, Mozzarella, and Pecorino Pizza

YIELD: 1 PIZZA • ACTIVE TIME: 20 MINUTES
TOTAL TIME: 30 MINUTES

Parmesan is the standard hard cheese used on pizzas, but here you want to use pecorino, as its saltiness is the perfect complement to the earthy mushrooms.

1 Preheat the oven to 550°F. Place the mushrooms, 1 tablespoon of the olive oil, and the garlic in a frying pan, season with salt and pepper, and cook over medium–high heat until the mushrooms release their liquid. Remove from heat and set aside.

2 Distribute 1 tablespoon of olive oil and the mozzarella over the pizza dough. Top with the sautéed mushrooms and garlic, sprinkle the Pecorino and parsley over everything, and season with salt and pepper.

3 Drizzle with the remaining olive oil, place in the oven, and cook until the crust is golden brown and the cheese is bubbly.

INGREDIENTS

1 cup wild mushrooms, chopped

3 tablespoons olive oil

1 garlic clove, minced

Salt and black pepper, to taste

1 ball of dough, stretched into a 10–inch round

¾ cup fresh mozzarella, drained and sliced

2 tablespoons pecorino cheese, grated

1 handful of parsley, chopped

Grilled Veggies and Tofu Cream Cheese Pizza

YIELD: 1 PIZZA • ACTIVE TIME: 15 MINUTES
TOTAL TIME: 35 MINUTES

While making a successful vegan pizza can seem daunting, this easy recipe will keep you and all the vegans in your life happy.

INGREDIENTS

1 zucchini, halved lengthwise

1 bell pepper, seeded and quartered

½ onion, halved

3 tablespoons olive oil

Salt and pepper, to taste

1½ tablespoons tofu cream cheese

1 ball of dough, stretched into a 10-inch round

⅓ cup tomato sauce, homemade (see page 129) or store-bought

1 handful of parsley, chopped

1 Preheat the oven to 550°F. Preheat your gas or charcoal grill to high heat.

2 Place the zucchini, pepper, and onion on the grill and cook for 5 to 6 minutes, until grill marks begin to show. Remove from the grill, transfer to a cutting board, and chop into bite-sized pieces. Place the vegetables in a bowl with 2 tablespoons of the olive oil, season with salt, and set aside. You can do this the day before, leaving the grilled vegetables to marinate in the fridge overnight.

3 Distribute dollops of the tofu cream cheese over the dough and then distribute the tomato sauce. Distribute the vegetables evenly over the pizza and sprinkle the parsley on top. Season with salt and pepper and drizzle with the remaining olive oil. Cook in the oven until the crust is golden brown, about 10 minutes.

Cherry Tomato and Pesto Pizza

YIELD: 1 PIZZA • ACTIVE TIME: 5 MINUTES
TOTAL TIME: 25 MINUTES

Nothing screams freshness like plump, delicious cherry tomatoes. Throw in the pesto and you're in for a real treat.

1 Preheat the oven to 550°F. Spread the pesto over the pizza dough. Distribute the mozzarella and then the cherry tomatoes over the pizza.

2 Sprinkle with the Parmesan, drizzle with the olive oil, and place in the oven. Cook until the crust is golden brown and the cheese is bubbly, about 10 minutes. Remove from oven and top with the basil leaves, if desired.

INGREDIENTS

⅓ cup Basil Pesto (see page 138)

1 ball of dough, stretched into a 10-inch round

¾ cup smoked mozzarella, sliced

6 to 8 cherry tomatoes, halved

1 tablespoon Parmesan cheese, grated

1 tablespoon olive oil

6 to 8 basil leaves (optional)

Mushroom and Artichoke Pan Pizza

**YIELD: 1 PIZZA • ACTIVE TIME: 40 MINUTES
TOTAL TIME: 2 HOURS**

Any wild mushroom will work on this pizza, but do your best to track down some chanterelles.

INGREDIENTS

2 tablespoons olive oil, plus more for greasing and drizzling

½ recipe of Basic Pizza Dough (see page 17)

1¼ cups chanterelle mushrooms, washed and roughly chopped

1 garlic clove, minced

1½ cups fresh mozzarella, drained and diced

1 handful of fresh parsley, chopped

½ cup artichokes, trimmed and sliced lengthwise

Sea salt, to taste

Buffalo mozzarella, drained and torn, for topping

1 Grease a 9 x 13–inch baking dish with olive oil and place the pizza dough in it. Working slowly and gently, spread the dough in the dish, stopping occasionally and allowing the dough to relax on its own. Cover with plastic wrap and let stand for 1 hour.

2 Place the 2 tablespoons of olive oil, the mushrooms, and the garlic in a large skillet and sauté over medium–high heat until the mushrooms begin to give up their moisture. Remove from heat and set aside.

3 Preheat the oven to 550°F. When the oven is ready, drizzle the dough with olive oil and place the dough on the bottom rack of the oven. Cook for 10 minutes, remove the dough from the oven, and lower the temperature to 430°F.

4 Distribute the mozzarella, parsley, mushrooms and garlic, and half of the artichokes over the dough. Season with salt and return to the oven, placing the dish on the middle rack this time. Bake until it looks golden (but not burned) and cooked through (but not dry), about 10 to 15 minutes. Remove from the oven, top with the remaining artichokes and the buffalo mozzarella, and serve.

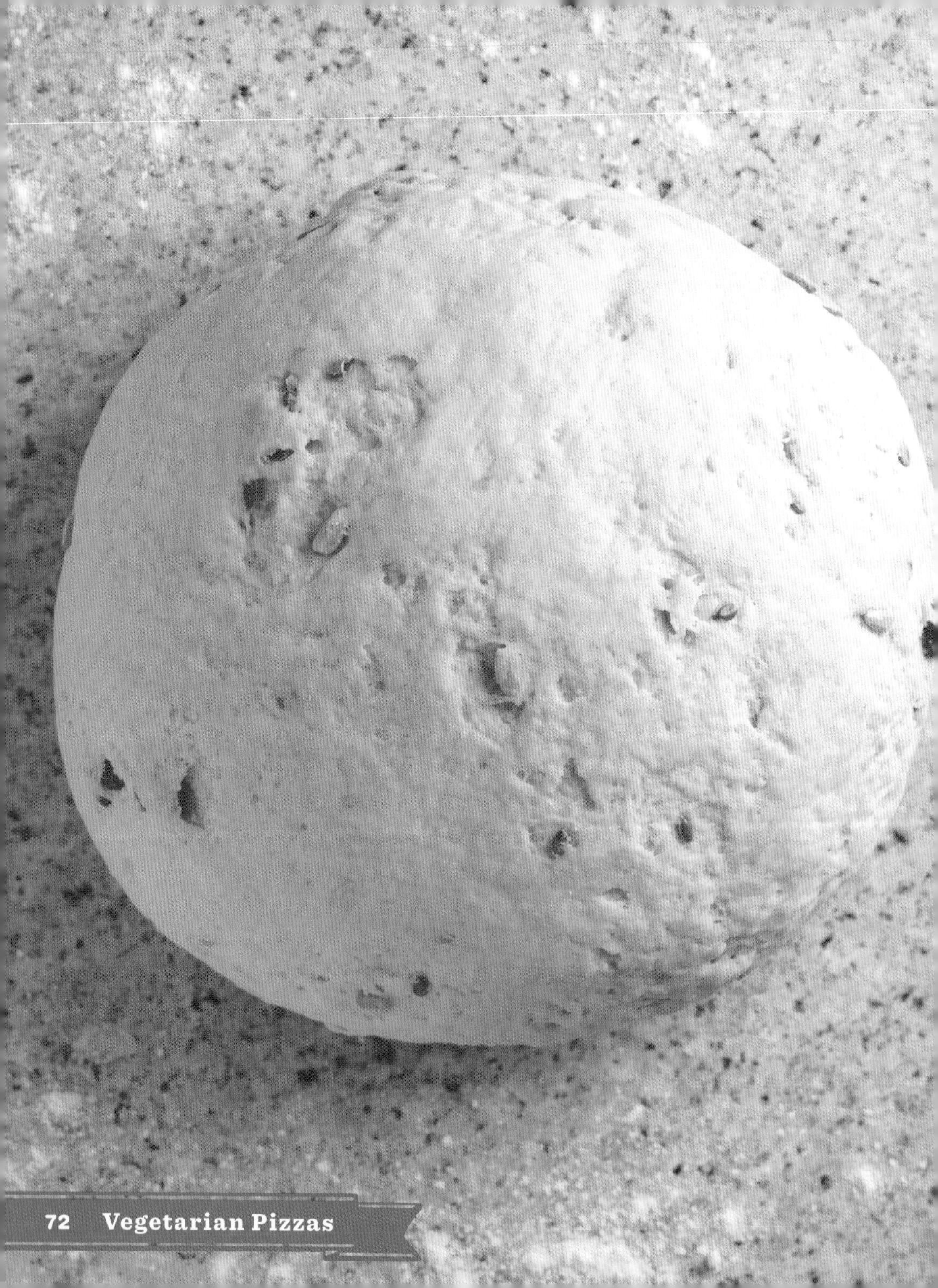

Bok Choy, Pine Nut, and Raisin Pizza

YIELD: 1 PIZZA • ACTIVE TIME: 20 MINUTES
TOTAL TIME: 30 MINUTES

Countering the slightly bitter taste of bok choy with the sweetness of raisins makes this inventive pizza something you can serve with confidence.

1 Preheat the oven to 550°F. Work the raisins and sunflower seeds into the ball of dough and then stretch it into a 10-inch round. Place 2 teaspoons of the olive oil in a large skillet and warm over medium–high heat. Add the bok choy and the garlic, season with salt, and cook until the bok choy has wilted.

2 Spread the tomato sauce over the pizza dough and top with the bok choy.

3 Sprinkle the pine nuts over the bok choy. Season with salt, drizzle with the remaining olive oil, and cook until the crust is golden brown, about 10 minutes.

INGREDIENTS

1 tablespoon raisins

1 tablespoon sunflower seeds

1 ball of dough

3 teaspoons olive oil

1½ cups bok choy, chopped

1 garlic clove, minced

Salt, to taste

⅓ cup tomato sauce, homemade (see page 129) or store–bought

1 tablespoon pine nuts

Melanzane Pizza

YIELD: 1 PIZZA • ACTIVE TIME: 20 MINUTES
TOTAL TIME: 50 MINUTES

Here's an easy way to enjoy two of Italy's favorite things: a Neapolitan pizza and thin slices of eggplant.

1 Place the slices of eggplant in a colander and lightly salt each layer. Let stand for 15 minutes.

2 Place the olive oil in a skillet and warm over medium heat. Add the eggplant and cook for 2 to 3 minutes on each side. Transfer to the refrigerator to cool.

3 Preheat oven to 480°F. Spread the crushed tomatoes over the dough and then distribute the basil leaves. Top with the mozzarella and then distribute the slices of eggplant evenly over the pizza.

4 Place the pizza in the oven and cook for approximately 15 minutes, until the crust is golden brown and the cheese is bubbly. Remove, top with the Parmesan, and serve.

INGREDIENTS

½ eggplant, sliced thin

Salt, to taste

2 tablespoons olive oil

1 (14 oz.) can of peeled San Marzano tomatoes, crushed by hand

1 ball of Neapolitan Pizza Dough (see page 18), stretched into a 10-inch round

3 to 4 basil leaves

½ cup fresh mozzarella cheese, drained and sliced thin

Parmesan cheese, grated, to taste

The Farmers Market

YIELD: 1 PIZZA • ACTIVE TIME: 40 to 50 MINUTES
TOTAL TIME: 1 HOUR

Yes, there's no sauce on this one, but the vegetables and the yogurt provide plenty of juiciness while keeping the incredible freshness at the forefront.

INGREDIENTS

2 tablespoons Greek yogurt

1 tablespoon chives, chopped

Squeeze of lemon juice

1 teaspoon chia seeds

1 ball of dough, stretched into a 10–inch round

¾ to 1 cup mozzarella, grated

½ cup red peppers, roasted and chopped

½ cup butternut squash, roasted and chopped

½ cup zucchini, roasted and chopped

½ cup beets, roasted and chopped

1 Preheat the oven to 480°F. In a small bowl, combine the Greek yogurt, chives, and lemon juice. Set aside.

2 Distribute the chia seeds in a circle on your baking stone or pizza pan and then place the dough on top of them. Press down so the seeds stick to the bottom.

3 Sprinkle the mozzarella over the dough and then top with the peppers, squash, zucchini, and beets.

4 Place in the oven and cook for 7 to 10 minutes, until the crust is golden brown and the cheese is bubbly. Remove and drizzle with the Greek yogurt mixture just before serving.

Tomato and Goat Cheese Pizza

YIELD: 1 PIZZA • ACTIVE TIME: 15 MINUTES
TOTAL TIME: 25 MINUTES

The tanginess and smooth texture of the goat cheese adds a delicious component to this classic pizza.

1 Preheat your oven to 550°F. Brush the dough with 1 tablespoon of the olive oil. Combine the goat cheese, basil, salt, and pepper in a small bowl and then spread this mixture on the dough. Top with the tomato slices and drizzle with the remaining olive oil.

2 Place the pizza on the top rack of the oven. Cook for about 8 minutes, until the crust is slightly golden. Turn on the broiler and cook for 2 minutes, until the cheese has melted.

INGREDIENTS

1 ball of dough, stretched into a 10-inch round

2 tablespoons olive oil

½ cup goat cheese

2 tablespoons basil leaves, chopped

Pinch of salt

Pinch of black pepper

1 large tomato, thinly sliced

Bite-Sized Zucchini Pizzas

YIELD: 4 SERVINGS • ACTIVE TIME: 20 MINUTES
TOTAL TIME: 25 MINUTES

These little "pizzas" are absolutely perfect for an appetizer at a summer cookout.

INGREDIENTS

½ cup butter, melted

2 garlic cloves, minced

2 large zucchinis, cut into rounds

½ cup tomato sauce, homemade (see page 129) or store-bought

½ cup mozzarella, grated

1 Preheat your gas or charcoal grill to medium heat. Combine the butter and garlic in a small bowl and set aside.

2 When the grill is 400°F to 450°F, place your zucchini slices on the grill and cook for about 2 minutes. Flip the slices over and brush with the butter–and–garlic mixture. Cook for 3 minutes, flip them over, and brush this side with the mixture.

3 Cover the slices with the tomato sauce, and mozzarella. Cook until the cheese is slightly melted, remove from the grill, and serve.

Portobello Pizzas

Earthy, spicy, and light, these mushroom–based "pizzas" make for a great dinner on a sweltering July night.

INGREDIENTS

¼ cup olive oil

4 garlic cloves, minced

2 tablespoons balsamic vinegar

8 large portobello mushroom caps, stemmed

1 cup tomato sauce, homemade (see page 129) or store–bought

1 cup mozzarella cheese, grated

½ cup Parmesan cheese, grated

½ cup spicy banana peppers, chopped

Basil leaves, for garnish

1 Place the oil, garlic, and vinegar in a large resealable bag and stir to combine. Place the mushroom caps in the bag and let them marinate for 1 hour.

2 Preheat your gas or charcoal grill to medium heat. Remove the mushroom caps from the bag and cover each one with the tomato sauce, mozzarella, Parmesan, and banana peppers.

3 When the grill is about 400°F to 450°F, place the caps on the grill and cook until the cheese is melted, about 10 minutes. Remove from heat, garnish with the basil leaves, and serve.

Pineapple Pizza

YIELD: 1 PIZZA • ACTIVE TIME: 15 MINUTES
TOTAL TIME: 25 MINUTES

Grilling the pineapple adds a caramelized quality that is absolute heaven when paired with the lightly charred crust that will result from cooking on the grill.

1 Place a baking stone on your grill and preheat the grill to high heat.

2 When the grill is 500°F, place the pineapple on the grill and cook until lightly charred, about 3 to 4 minutes. Remove from the grill, transfer to a cutting board, and cut into bite-sized cubes. Set aside.

3 Spread 1 tablespoon of the olive oil over the dough. Spread the sauce on the dough and then distribute the mozzarella and pineapple evenly over the pizza. Sprinkle with the cilantro, season with salt, and place the pizza on the baking stone. Cook until the crust is golden brown and the cheese is bubbly, about 10 minutes. Drizzle with the remaining olive oil before serving.

INGREDIENTS

½ cup fresh pineapple slices, sliced

2 tablespoons olive oil

1 ball of dough, stretched into a 10-inch round

½ cup tomato sauce, homemade (see page 129) or store-bought

5 oz. mozzarella, grated

2 tablespoons cilantro, chopped

Salt, to taste

Flatbreads

While pizza has taken over the West, it is only one of the delicious flatbreads enjoyed across the globe. Because of both taste and versatility, the flatbread has become a fundamental piece of cuisines everywhere, a phenomenon that's easy to understand once you've tried them all.

Featuring everything from Flour Tortillas (see page 88) to the Knäckebröd (see page 118) that Swedes feel is an essential piece of any smörgåsbord, you'll soon see why we're convinced that the world (of food) is flat.

Flour Tortillas

YIELD: 12 TORTILLAS • ACTIVE TIME: 30 MINUTES
TOTAL TIME: 40 MINUTES

While you can always pick tortillas up at the store, those are a world away from what you can whip up in the comfort of your home.

INGREDIENTS

3 cups all-purpose flour, plus more for dusting

1 teaspoon salt

2 teaspoons baking powder

4 tablespoons butter, chilled

1½ cups water, at room temperature

1 Place the flour in a large bowl. Add the salt and baking powder and stir to combine.

2 Add the butter and use your hands to blend it into the mixture until you have a crumbly dough. Add 1 cup of the water, work it in with your hands, and then gradually add the remaining ½ cup. Incorporate until you have a dough that is smooth and not too sticky.

3 Lightly flour a work surface and turn out the dough. Knead until it's soft and elastic, about 10 minutes. Divide into 12 equal pieces and use a lightly floured rolling pin to roll each piece out into 10-inch rounds.

4 Heat a cast-iron skillet over high heat and add a tortilla. Cook for just 15 seconds on each side, stack them on a plate, and cover with a tea towel. Serve warm.

Corn Tortillas

Flour tortillas are the standard nowadays, but the authentic Mexican version utilizes a corn flour known as masa harina.

1 In a large bowl, add the flour and the salt and stir to combine. Cover with boiling water and stir with a spoon until combined.

2 When the mixture is cool enough to handle, work it into a large ball of dough. If the consistency is too dry, add more water; if too sticky, add more masa harina.

3 Heat a cast–iron skillet over medium–high heat. Working with one small ball of the dough at a time, use something heavy (such as a cookbook) to flatten it into a thin disk between two layers of parchment paper. Place the flattened tortillas in the skillet and cook for 30 seconds on each side, until brown spots begin appear. Stack the cooked tortillas on a plate and cover with a tea towel.

INGREDIENTS

3 cups masa harina, plus more as needed

¾ teaspoons salt

1¾ cups boiling water, plus more as needed

Chicken Fajitas

YIELD: 6 TO 8 SERVINGS • ACTIVE TIME: 30 MINUTES
TOTAL TIME: 5 HOURS

The trick is to bring this dish to the table while the meat and veggies are still sizzling, as it adds a real wow factor.

INGREDIENTS

For the Chicken

½ cup orange juice

Juice of 1 lime

4 garlic cloves, minced

1 jalapeño pepper, seeded and diced

2 tablespoons fresh cilantro, chopped

1 teaspoon cumin

1 teaspoon dried oregano

Salt and pepper, to taste

3 tablespoons olive oil

3 to 4 boneless, skinless chicken breasts, cut into strips

For the Vegetables

2 tablespoons olive oil

1 red onion, sliced thin

1 red bell pepper, seeded and sliced thin

1 green bell pepper, seeded and sliced thin

1 yellow bell pepper, seeded and sliced thin

2 jalapeño peppers, seeded and sliced thin

3 garlic cloves, minced

¼ cup freshly squeezed lime juice

¼ cup cilantro, chopped

Salt and pepper, to taste

1 Prepare the chicken. In a bowl, add the orange juice, lime juice, garlic, jalapeño, cilantro, cumin, oregano, salt, and pepper. When thoroughly combined, add the olive oil. Place the chicken pieces into the mixture, stir to coat, cover the bowl with plastic wrap, and refrigerate for about 4 hours.

2 Heat a cast–iron skillet over medium–high heat. Remove the chicken from the marinade and place in the skillet. Cook, while stirring and turning the pieces over, until they are cooked through, about 8 to 10 minutes. Transfer the cooked chicken to a platter and cover loosely with foil.

3 Prepare the vegetables. Reduce the heat to medium, add the olive oil, onion, bell peppers, jalapeño, and garlic. Cook, while stirring, for 3 to 5 minutes until the vegetables have softened. Add the lime juice and cilantro and cook for 2 to 3 minutes. Season with salt and pepper.

4 While the vegetables are still sizzling, push them to one side of the pan and put the chicken on the other side. Serve immediately.

Note: You'll want to serve these fajitas alongside Flour Tortillas (see page 88), Guacamole (see page 97), Pico de Gallo (see page 97), sour cream, and sliced jalapeño peppers. Prepare these while waiting for the chicken to finish marinating.

Breakfast Tacos

YIELD: 6 TACOS • ACTIVE TIME: 20 MINUTES
TOTAL TIME: 1 HOUR AND 20 MINUTES

These tacos are sure to brighten everyone's morning.

1 Prepare the Pico de Gallo. Combine all of the ingredients in a bowl. Refrigerate for 1 hour to let the flavors mingle.

2 Prepare the Guacamole. Place all of the ingredients in a small bowl, stir to combine, and set aside.

3 Prepare the tacos. Heat the oil in a cast-iron skillet over medium heat. In a separate bowl, combine the eggs, spices, and cilantro.

4 Place the egg mixture in the skillet and scramble until the eggs are cooked through.

5 Serve with the warm tortillas, Pico de Gallo, Guacamole, and other fixings of your choice.

INGREDIENTS

For the Pico de Gallo

4 Roma or plum tomatoes, diced
1 jalapeño pepper, diced
½ red onion
¼ cilantro, chopped
Zest and juice of ½ a lime
Salt, to taste

For the Guacamole

Meat from 2 ripe avocados, smashed
2 tablespoons cilantro, chopped
2 tablespoons red onion, minced
Zest and juice of ½ lime
1 tablespoon jalapeño pepper, minced
Salt, to taste

For the Tacos

2 tablespoons vegetable oil
8 eggs
1 tablespoon chili powder
1 tablespoon cumin
½ tablespoon adobo seasoning
1 tablespoon dried oregano
2 tablespoons cilantro, chopped
6 Corn Tortillas (see page 91), warmed

Grilled Veggie Quesadillas

YIELD: 4 SERVINGS • ACTIVE TIME: 20 MINUTES
TOTAL TIME: 40 MINUTES

Quesadillas tend to be disappointing, as the continually soggy product fails to live up to the mouthwatering concept. Preparing them on the grill solves that problem and allows you to move beyond abstract enjoyment.

INGREDIENTS

2 large green zucchini, cut into ¼ inch–thick rounds

2 large yellow squash, cut into ¼ inch–thick rounds

Salt and pepper, to taste

2 red bell peppers, seeded and sliced

2 orange bell peppers, seeded and sliced

1 medium red onion, sliced

8 tablespoons Basil Pesto (see page 138)

1 cup cheddar cheese

4 Flour Tortillas (see page 88)

1 Preheat your gas or charcoal grill to medium heat. While you are waiting, season the zucchini and squash with salt and pepper.

2 When the grill is about 400°F, place the vegetables on the grill and cook until they have softened and become lightly charred, about 8 to 10 minutes. Remove from the grill and set aside.

3 Divide the pesto, vegetables, and cheese evenly between the tortillas. Fold the tortillas over and then grill for 3 minutes on each side. Remove from grill, cut into wedges, and serve.

Tip: Serve with Guacamole (see page 97), salsa, and lime wedges.

Veggie Tacos with Avocado Crema

YIELD: 6 TO 8 SERVINGS • ACTIVE TIME: 15 TO 20 MINUTES
TOTAL TIME: 45 MINUTES

The silky smooth Avocado Crema transforms these simple veggie tacos into something luxurious.

1 Preheat your gas or charcoal grill to medium–high heat. Place the vegetables, olive oil, garlic, cumin, and salt in a large bowl and stir to combine.

2 Lay out 6 piceces of aluminum foil, divide the vegetable mixture between the pieces of foil, and fold to create sealed packets.

3 When the grill is 450°F, place the packets on the grill and cook until tender, about 20 to 25 minutes.

4 While the vegetables are roasting, prepare the Avocado Crema. Place all ingredients in a blender and puree until smooth. Set aside.

5 Serve the grilled vegetables alongside the Avocado Crema, Corn Tortillas, cheddar cheese, and, if desired, serrano peppers.

INGREDIENTS

For the Tacos

1 small zucchini, diced

1 small summer squash, diced

½ medium red onion, diced

Kernels from 1 ear of sweet corn

1 cup cherry tomatoes, halved

2 tablespoons olive oil

2 garlic cloves, minced

2 teaspoons cumin

¼ teaspoon salt

Corn Tortillas (see page 91), warmed, for serving

Cheddar cheese, shredded, for serving

2 serrano peppers, chopped, for serving (optional)

For the Avocado Crema

Meat from 1 avocado

⅓ cup plain Greek yogurt

¼ cup cilantro, minced

1 tablespoon lime juice

Arepas

This traditional corn flatbread is commonly eaten in Venezuela and Colombia. It can be eaten with a dip or split and filled like a sandwich.

INGREDIENTS

4 cups masa harina

1⅔ cups water

1 teaspoon salt

Vegetable oil, for frying

1 Place all of the ingredients in a large bowl and mix until a smooth dough forms. Cover and let the dough rest for 30 minutes.

2 Preheat the oven to 400°F. Roll the dough out to $^4/_5$ inch thickness and cut 6 to 7 disks out of it.

3 Coat the bottom of a cast–iron skillet with vegetable oil. Place the arepas in the oil and fry for 2 minutes on each side. Remove and transfer to a paper towel–lined plate.

4 When all of the arepas have been fried, place them on a baking sheet and bake for 10 minutes.

5 Remove and cut away any irregularities, making each arepa as close as possible to a circle.

6 Heat the skillet over medium–high heat and cook one arepa at a time for a few minutes on each side. Serve warm.

Pita Bread

YIELD: 16 PITAS • ACTIVE TIME: 1 HOUR
TOTAL TIME: 2 HOURS AND 15 MINUTES

After originating in Greece, this versatile bread has made its way around the world.

1 Combine the yeast and the water in a bowl. Let sit for about 10 minutes until foamy. Add the yeast mixture to a large bowl. Add the all–purpose flour and stir until a stiff dough forms. Cover and let the dough rise for about 1 hour.

2 Add 1 tablespoon of the oil and salt to the dough and then stir in the whole wheat flour in 1/2–cup increments. Stir until the dough is soft. Turn out onto a lightly floured surface and knead it until it is smooth and elastic, about 10 minutes. Coat the bottom and sides of a large mixing bowl with butter. Place the ball of dough in the bowl, cover loosely with plastic wrap, place in a naturally warm, draft–free location, and let it rise until doubled in size, about 45 minutes to 1 hour.

3 On a lightly floured surface, punch down the dough and cut into 16 pieces. Put the pieces on a baking sheet and cover with a dish towel while working with individual pieces. Roll out each piece with a rolling pin until it is approximately 7 inches in diameter. Stack them between sheets of plastic wrap.

4 Heat a cast–iron skillet over high heat and add the remaining olive oil. Cook each pita for about 20 seconds on one side, then flip and cook for a minute on the other side, until bubbles form. Turn again and cook until the pita puffs up, another minute or so. Store under a tea towel until ready to serve.

INGREDIENTS

2¼ teaspoons active dry yeast

2½ cups water (110°F to 115°F)

3 cups all–purpose flour, plus more for dusting

2 tablespoons olive oil

1 tablespoon salt

3 cups whole wheat flour

Grilled Kale and Feta Pita

**YIELD: 4 SERVINGS • ACTIVE TIME: 10 MINUTES
TOTAL TIME: 15 MINUTES**

It can be tough to use all of the kale you buy for your smoothies. But once you get this recipe down, your days of throwing out spoiled greens will be over.

INGREDIENTS

2 tablespoons olive oil

1 red onion, minced

2 garlic cloves, minced

6 oz. kale, shredded

7 oz. feta cheese, crumbled

½ cup cheddar cheese, shredded

Pinch of paprika

4 pieces of Pita Bread (see page 105)

2 lemons, cut into wedges

1 Place the half of the olive oil, the onion, garlic, kale, feta, cheddar, and paprika in a large bowl and mix until well combined.

2 Spread about half of the mixture over one of the pita breads and place another pita on top. Repeat this with the other half of the filling and the other two pieces of pita. Preheat your gas or charcoal grill to medium–high heat.

3 Before placing the pizza on the grill, brush the exposed side of the pitas with the remaining olive oil. Grill, while turning, for about 3 to 4 minutes or until they begin to crisp and turn a nice golden color. Compress with a metal spatula as they cook.

4 Remove from heat when pitas reach desired crispness and cut into wedges. Squeeze lemon over the pita and serve.

Naan

YIELD: 8 NAAN • ACTIVE TIME: 30 MINUTES
TOTAL TIME: 3 HOURS

Naan is the most common type of leavened bread in both Central and Southern Asia. While it is generally baked in a tandoor–style oven, it can also be cooked in a frying pan, like the version below.

1 Dissolve the yeast in the water and let rest for 5 minutes.

2 In a large bowl, combine the yeast mixture with the rest of the ingredients, except for the salted butter. Start working the dough, either with a standing mixer or by hand until it feels smooth. This should take about 10 minutes.

3 Let the dough rest, covered, in a naturally warm spot and let it rise for 1 to 1½ hours.

4 Transfer the dough to a clean and floured surface, divide in 8 pieces, and shape into rounds. Place the rounds on a tray covered with parchment paper and let rest, covered, for 30 to 45 minutes.

5 Warm a greased cast–iron skillet or frying pan over medium–high heat.

6 Take one round at a time and flatten it thin. Cook on both sides until some browned bubbles form on both surfaces. Brush with melted, hot butter when still hot and serve.

INGREDIENTS

1 teaspoon active dry yeast

½ cup water (100°F)

2¾ cups all-purpose flour, plus more for dusting

½ cup plain yogurt

3 tablespoons vegetable oil

Salted butter, melted

Authentic Injera

YIELD: 10 TO 12 INJERA • ACTIVE TIME: 30 MINUTES
TOTAL TIME: 2 TO 3 DAYS

Letting the dough ferment for a few days improves the flavor along with the nutritional properties of this traditional Ethiopian bread.

INGREDIENTS

3 cups teff flour

5⅓ cups water, plus more as needed

1 teaspoon salt

1 tablespoon vegetable oil

1 In a large bowl, combine the flour with 4 cups of the water. Cover with plastic wrap and let rest at room temperature for 2 to 3 days. The batter is ready when bubbles have formed and the mixture has a sour smell.

2 Do not stir. Pour out as much of the water as possible, being careful not to pour out the wet flour on the bottom. Bring the remaining water to boil in a small saucepan.

3 Take 1½ cups of the fermented batter and place it in the boiling water, stirring vigorously, until it thickens.

4 Incorporate the thickened batter into the original batter and stir well.

5 Add the salt and stir until the mixture reaches the consistency of a pancake batter. Add more water if necessary.

6 Heat a cast–iron skillet or shallow frying pan over medium heat. Place the oil in the pan and pour enough batter to cover the whole surface of the skillet, as you would do for a crepe, but slightly thicker.

7 After 2 minutes, cover with a lid and cook until bubbles have formed and the bottom side of the injera detaches easily from the pan. Place parchment paper between cooked injera so they do not stick together.

Injera with Yeast

YIELD: 15 INJERA • ACTIVE TIME: 30 MINUTES
TOTAL TIME: 4½ HOURS

This is a quicker version of the delicious Ethiopian bread that is generally fermented for several days. If you're pressed for time and craving Ethiopian food, this recipe gives you a good approximation of the real thing.

INGREDIENTS

3 teaspoons active dry yeast

2⅔ cups water (100°F to 105°F)

⅓ cups teff flour

1 teaspoon salt

1 tablespoon vegetable oil

1 Dissolve the yeast in the water and let rest for 5 minutes. In a large bowl, combine the yeast mixture with the flour. Cover with plastic wrap and let rest for 3 to 4 hours.

2 Whisk in the salt. Place the oil in a cast–iron skillet and warm over medium heat.

3 Pour in enough batter to cover the whole surface of the skillet, as you would do for a crepe, but slightly thicker.

4 After 2 minutes, cover with a lid and cook until bubbles have formed and the bottom side of the injera detaches easily from the pan. Place parchment paper between cooked injera so they do not stick together.

Lefse

YIELD: 12 LEFSE • ACTIVE TIME: 20 MINUTES
TOTAL TIME: ABOUT 40 MINUTES

This potato–based flatbread has become popular in the United States thanks to the concentration of Norwegian immigrants in the Midwest. The recipe below is adapted to require no special tools.

1 Bring water to boil in a large saucepan and add the potatoes. Cook until tender. Drain, transfer the potatoes to a bowl, and add the butter. Use a fork to mash the potatoes.

2 Add half of the flour and knead until a dough forms.

3 Transfer the dough to a clean surface and add the remaining flour a little bit at a time. Incorporate the flour, stopping if you reach a consistency that allows you to roll the dough.

4 Form the dough into a ball and divide into 12 pieces. Roll each piece into a round and flatten into a thin disk. Use flour to prevent the dough from sticking.

5 Heat a cast–iron skillet over medium–high heat. Roll one disk at a time around a floured rolling pin and transfer it to the pan. Cook for 2 minutes on each side, set on a paper towel, and repeat with the remaining lefse.

INGREDIENTS

2 cups starchy potatoes, peeled and cubed

⅓ cup butter

1½ cups flour, plus more for dusting

½ teaspoon salt

Roti

This is one of the great flatbreads that are a staple of Indian cuisine. Also known as chapati, it is crucial to find the right whole wheat flour for this recipe.

INGREDIENTS

2½ cups finely ground whole wheat flour

1 tablespoon vegetable oil, plus 1 teaspoon

1 teaspoon salt

1 cup water

1 In a large bowl, combine the flour, oil, salt, and ³/₄ of the water. Work the dough by hand until a soft, but not sticky, dough forms. Add the remaining water as needed, a little bit at a time. Knead the dough for 10 minutes, cover, and let rest for 1 hour.

2 Transfer to a clean surface and divide the dough into 15 pieces. Heat a cast–iron skillet over medium–high heat. Working with one piece at a time, flatten into a thin disk and transfer to the frying pan. Cook for 30 seconds on each side and press down on the bread to cause it to puff up.

3 Cover with aluminum foil and repeat with the remaining roti.

Tunnbröd

YIELD: 12 TUNNBROD • ACTIVE TIME: 30 MINUTES
TOTAL TIME: 2½ HOURS

In Sweden this bread is sold on the streets filled with steamy hot mashed potatoes, sausage, and mustard. They are also lovely with a soft cheese spread and smoked salmon or cold cuts.

1 Dissolve the yeast in the milk and let rest 5 minutes. In a large bowl, combine the mixture with the flours, the molasses, and the crushed seeds. Knead the mixture until a dough forms. Add the butter in pieces, continuing to work the dough, and incorporate the salt toward the end of the kneading (about 10 minutes).

2 Let the dough rest, covered, in a warm spot until it looks fully risen. This should take about 1 to 1½ hours.

3 Divide the dough in 12 pieces and roll each piece into a round. Place the rounds on parchment paper, cover, and let rest for 1 hour.

4 On a lightly floured surface, use a rolling pin to roll one round at a time into a ⅕ inch–thick disk. Use a fork to make some shallow holes on the top of each disk.

5 Warm a cast–iron skillet over medium–high heat and cook one disk at a time for 2 to 3 minutes on each side, until browned.

INGREDIENTS

2½ teaspoons active dry yeast

1½ cups milk, warmed (100°F to 105°F)

2¼ cups all–purpose flour, plus more for dusting

1 cup graham flour

¾ cup rye flour

2⅓ tablespoons light molasses

1 teaspoon fennel or anise seeds, crushed

4 tablespoons butter

1 teaspoon salt

Knäckebröd

YIELD: 12 KNÄCKEBRÖD • ACTIVE TIME: 50 MINUTES
TOTAL TIME: 2½ HOURS

Knäckebröd means crispy bread in Swedish and they are a fixture at any smörgåsbord. They stay fresh for a long time and can accompany a variety of foods.

INGREDIENTS

1¾ teaspoons active dry yeast

1⅓ cups water

1 tablespoon whole caraway seeds

½ cup light rye flour

2⅔ cups bread flour

½ cup all-purpose flour, plus more for dusting

1 cup sesame seeds

1½ teaspoons salt

1 In a large bowl, dissolve the yeast in the water and add the caraway seeds. Let rest for 15 minutes.

2 Add all the other ingredients and knead until a dough forms, about 10 minutes. Cover and let rest for about 1½ hours.

3 Roll the dough into a long log and cut it into 12 pieces. Form each piece into a round, place on parchment paper, cover, and let rest for 40 minutes.

4 Preheat the oven to 550°F. On a lightly floured surface, flatten one round at a time with a rolling pin, making it as thin as possible without tearing the dough. Use a fork to poke shallow holes on top of each round.

5 Working with a couple of rounds at a time, place them on a baking sheet and cook until they are slightly browned and look crunchy, about 10 minutes. Cover and repeat until all the rounds have been baked.

Schuttelbrot

This crunchy flatbread hails from Northern Italy, where it became popular because it could last through the long winters when food was scarce.

1 Dissolve the yeast in the water and let rest for 5 minutes. In a large bowl, combine the yeast mixture with the rest of the ingredients. Knead the mixture until a dough forms, about 15 minutes. Cover and let rest for 30 minutes.

2 Roll into a long log and cut it into 8 pieces. Form each piece into a round, place on parchment paper, cover, and let rest for 1 hour.

3 On a floured surface, use your hands to flatten one round at a time, working as if you were stretching a pizza dough. You need to reach a thickness of ⅕ inch. Use a rolling pin if using your hands feels too difficult. Cover the disks and let rest for 15 to 20 minutes.

4 Place a baking stone in the oven and preheat the oven to 410°F.

5 Place the rounds on the stone and bake for 20 minutes, or until lightly browned.

INGREDIENTS

2½ teaspoons active dry yeast

1½ cups water (100°F to 105°F)

3⅗ cups medium rye flour

1½ cups all-purpose flour

2 teaspoons seeds (mix of fennel, caraway, coriander, anise)

1½ teaspoons salt

1 teaspoon sugar

3¼ tablespoons buttermilk

Piadina

Piadina is a flatbread traditional to Central Italy. Generally paired with cold cuts and cheese, it is delicious if grilled after being filled.

INGREDIENTS

4½ cups all-purpose flour

1 cup water

4 tablespoons lard

1 teaspoon baking soda

1 teaspoon salt

1 In a large bowl, combine all the ingredients. Knead the mixture for 10 minutes until a dough forms. Cover and let rest for 30 minutes.

2 Divide the dough in 7 pieces, shape into rounds, and roll into thin disks. Make each disk even by cutting any irregularities away, making it as close as possible to a perfect circle.

3 Warm a cast-iron skillet over medium-high heat. Working with one disk at a time, cook for a couple of minutes on each side, until it is browned all over.

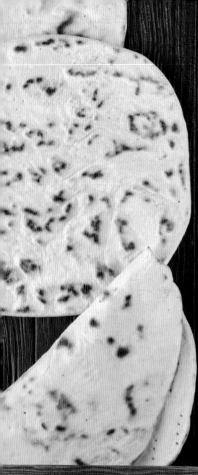

Sauces

The various flavors that pizzas and flatbreads can accommodate are a huge part of their popularity around the globe. With this in mind, we've supplied you with a number of easy–to–prepare, delicious sauces that can transform your disks of dough.

Some of these sauces, like the Tomato and Eggplant Sauce alla Norma (see page 131) or the Roasted Poblano Pepper Sauce (see page 142), are so good that you may find yourself not even bothering with cheese or toppings. Yes, there is an exceptional recipe for Classic Fresh Tomato Sauce (see page 129), but you should experiment with as many of these as you can.

Tomato Concasse: A number of recipes call for you to remove the skin and seeds from a tomato, as they can be bitter. To do this easily, boil enough water for a tomato to be submerged and add a pinch of salt. Prepare an ice bath and score the top of the tomato with a paring knife. Place the tomato in the boiling water for 30 seconds, carefully remove it, and place it in the ice bath. Once the tomato is cool, remove from ice bath and peel with the paring knife. Cut into quarters and remove the seeds.

Classic Fresh Tomato Sauce

YIELD: 4 SERVINGS • ACTIVE TIME: 20 MINUTES
TOTAL TIME: 45 MINUTES

If you're going to the trouble of making sauce from fresh tomatoes, you probably don't want your freezer involved. This recipe deals with such a small quantity of fresh tomatoes that it's quick, easy, and only makes enough for a few pizzas.

1 Place the tomatoes in a food processor or blender and puree them.

2 Heat a large skillet over low heat for 2 to 3 minutes. Add the olive oil (or butter), raise the heat to medium, and heat for 1 or 2 minutes. Add the onion and a pinch of salt and cook, stirring frequently, until softened, about 10 minutes. Add the tomatoes and two pinches of salt and stir. Bring to a boil, reduce the heat to low, cover, and simmer until thickened, about 20 minutes.

3 Once the sauce is done, place the whole basil leaves, if using, on the surface and close the lid for 5 minutes. The basil will gently perfume the sauce.

Note: If you can't find fresh tomatoes, just substitute a 28 oz. can of pureed San Marzano tomatoes for the plum tomatoes and skip Step 1.

INGREDIENTS

4 pounds very ripe plum tomatoes, concasse and chopped

2 tablespoons extra virgin olive oil or unsalted butter

1 medium onion, grated or thinly sliced

Salt, to taste

1 handful of basil leaves (optional)

Roasted Tomato and Garlic Sauce

YIELD: 4 SERVINGS • ACTIVE TIME: 15 MINUTES
TOTAL TIME: 2 HOURS

Garlic can be a bit overpowering in most simple tomato sauce recipes; however, the earthy sweetness of roasted garlic makes this recipe a tasty exception.

INGREDIENTS

3 pounds very ripe plum tomatoes, halved lengthwise

¼ cup extra virgin olive oil, plus more as needed

5 large garlic cloves

Salt and black pepper, to taste

1 handful of basil leaves

1 Preheat the oven to 350°F. Place the tomatoes on a large parchment–lined baking sheet and drizzle with the olive oil. Using your fingers, mix well to ensure an even coating. Arrange the tomatoes cut side down, put the sheet on the center rack, lower the temperature to 325°F, and roast for 1 hour.

2 After 1 hour, remove the baking sheet, place the garlic in a small bowl, and drizzle with enough oil to lightly coat them. Add the garlic to the baking sheet and roast for another 30 minutes. Remove from the oven, season with salt and pepper, and let cool. Once cool enough to handle, remove the skins from the garlic cloves.

3 Place the tomatoes, garlic, and basil leaves in a blender or food processor and puree until smooth. When ready to use, transfer to a medium saucepan over medium heat and heat until gently bubbling.

Tomato and Eggplant Sauce alla Norma

YIELD: 4 SERVINGS • ACTIVE TIME: 40 MINUTES
TOTAL TIME: 1½ HOURS

From Sicily's ancient port city of Catania, this traditional sauce features a trifecta of the island's renowned ingredients: tomatoes, eggplant, and ricotta, which perfectly balances out the natural acidity in the tomatoes.

1 If the centers of the eggplants are overly seedy or spongy, remove those sections, as they will not help the texture and flavor of the sauce. Cut the eggplant quarters into 1–inch cubes, put in a colander, and sprinkle with 2 tablespoons of salt. Let drain for 30 minutes and then thoroughly pat the cubes dry with paper towels.

2 Preheat the oven to 400°F. Place the eggplant cubes in a large baking dish, add the olive oil and, using your hands, toss the eggplant and oil together until all the cubes are evenly coated. Spread the cubes into an even layer, place the dish on the center rack and roast, gently stirring twice during roasting, until they are tender and golden brown, about 25 minutes. Remove from the oven and set aside.

3 When ready to use, place the eggplant cubes, tomato sauce, and ricotta cheese in a large saucepan, stir to combine, and cook over medium heat until heated through. Season with salt and pepper before serving.

INGREDIENTS

2 medium, firm eggplants, peeled and quartered

2 tablespoons salt, plus more to taste

5 tablespoons extra virgin olive oil

5 cups Classic Fresh Tomato Sauce (see page 129)

1 cup ricotta cheese

Freshly ground black pepper, to taste

Arrabbiata

Arrabbiata translates to "angry," and this spicy sauce is sure to get your taste buds agitated—in a good way.

1 Heat a large, deep skillet over low heat for 1 to 2 minutes. Add the olive oil, garlic, and chilies, raise the heat to medium–low, and cook until the garlic begins to turn golden, 1 to 2 minutes. Remove the garlic and as much of the chilies as possible, discard, and then add the tomatoes, breaking them up with your hands as you add them to the skillet (also add any liquid from the can). Raise the heat to medium–high and bring to a boil. Reduce the heat to medium–low and cook, while stirring occasionally, until the sauce is thick and the oil is on the surface, about 20 minutes.

2 Add parsley and season with salt and pepper before serving.

INGREDIENTS

2 tablespoons extra virgin olive oil

3 garlic cloves, crushed

2 dried chilies, chopped

1 (28 oz.) can of peeled San Marzano tomatoes

1 handful of parsley, leaves removed and chopped

Salt and black pepper, to taste

Puttanesca Sauce

This is reputed to have been invented by "ladies of the night" who wanted to lure unwitting customers into their lairs. Take just one whiff of this aromatic sauce and the legend will seem more than plausible.

INGREDIENTS

½ cup extra virgin olive oil

3 garlic cloves, minced

1 (28 oz.) can of peeled San Marzano tomatoes, crushed by hand

½ pound black olives, pitted

¼ cup nonpareil capers

5 oil–packed anchovy fillets or 2 whole salt–packed anchovies

1 teaspoon red pepper flakes

Salt and black pepper, to taste

1 Place a large, deep skillet over low heat for 2 minutes. Add the olive oil and garlic and increase the heat to medium–low. Cook the garlic until it begins to sizzle gently, add the tomatoes and their juice, olives, capers, and anchovies and stir while pressing down on the anchovies to break them up.

2 Add the red pepper flakes, season with salt and pepper, stir to combine, and raise the heat to medium. Simmer, while stirring occasionally, until the sauce thickens slightly, about 10 minutes.

Bolognese Sauce

YIELD: 10 SERVINGS • ACTIVE TIME: 20 MINUTES
TOTAL TIME: 4½ HOURS

Recipes for this rich meat sauce from the beautiful city of Bologna often include carrots; however, to enhance the sauce's savory flavor, it is better to omit them. The natural sugars of the carrots throw off the balance of the ingredients, making the sauce too sweet.

1 Heat a large heavy–bottomed pot over medium–low heat for 2 to 3 minutes. Add the olive oil and raise the heat to medium–high. Heat the oil for a couple of minutes, then add the onion, celery, and a couple of pinches of salt, and stir. When the vegetables begin to sizzle, reduce the heat to low, cover, and cook for 30 minutes, while stirring occasionally.

2 Raise the heat to medium–high and add the ground meat. With a potato masher or wooden spoon, press down on it to break up large chunks. When the meat has turned a grayish brown and there is no pink remaining, add the milk. Continue cooking, while stirring occasionally, until the milk has completely evaporated.

3 Add the tomatoes, bay leaves, cloves, and a few pinches of salt, stir, and bring to a boil. Reduce the heat to low and cook, uncovered, for 4 hours, stirring every 30 minutes or so. You should see a gentle bubbling in the pot. You'll know the sauce is done when it has visibly thickened and the fat has separated. Discard the bay leaves before using.

INGREDIENTS

3 tablespoons extra virgin olive oil

1 medium yellow onion, grated

2 celery stalks and fronds, grated

Salt, to taste

2 pounds ground meat (blend of pork, veal, and beef)

2 cups whole milk

2 (28 oz.) cans of peeled San Marzano tomatoes, pureed

2 bay leaves

7 cloves or 1 teaspoon ground cloves

Basil Pesto

YIELD: 4 SERVINGS • ACTIVE TIME: 25 MINUTES
TOTAL TIME: 25 MINUTES

The seaside region of Liguria has made many delectable contributions to Italian cooking, including focaccia. But this simple pesto is the most famous of them all.

INGREDIENTS

¼ cup walnuts or pine nuts

2 large garlic cloves, peeled

Sea salt, to taste

2 cups basil, tightly packed

½ cup extra virgin olive oil

¼ cup pecorino Romano cheese, grated

¼ cup Parmesan cheese, grated

1 Heat a small skillet over low heat for 1 minute. Add the nuts and cook, while stirring frequently, until either they begin to give off a toasty fragrance (if using walnuts), or until they become lightly golden brown (if using pine nuts), approximately 2 to 3 minutes. Transfer to a plate to cool.

2 Place the nuts, garlic, and salt in a food processor or blender and pulse until crushed and crumbly looking. Add the basil and pulse until finely minced. Transfer the mixture to a medium bowl and add the oil in a thin stream as you quickly whisk it in. Do not add the oil to the food processor or blender, as the oil becomes bitter when processed.

3 Add the cheeses and stir to thoroughly combine. Use or store in an airtight container, covered with a thin film of olive oil, in the refrigerator for up to 3 months.

Variation: Substituting toasted hazelnuts and Manchego cheese will inject even more nuttiness into your pesto.

Chipotle and Pistachio Pesto

This sauce, as you might expect, is robust and needs to be paired with a subtle, nutty cheese such as Manchego.

1 Place the chipotles and garlic in a food processor or blender and puree until smooth. Add the pistachios and pulse 5 or 6 times until slightly crushed. Transfer the mixture to a medium bowl and add the oil in a slow, steady stream while whisking continuously.

2 Add the Manchego, season with salt, and stir to combine.

INGREDIENTS

4 canned chipotle peppers in adobo sauce, seeded

3 garlic cloves, peeled

⅔ cup salted pistachios, shelled

⅓ cup grapeseed oil

1 cup Manchego cheese, freshly grated

Salt, to taste

Roasted Poblano Pepper Sauce

YIELD: 4 SERVINGS • ACTIVE TIME: 1 HOUR
TOTAL TIME: 1½ HOURS

This recipe fuses the subtle smoky quality of roasted poblanos, the sweetness of corn and caramelized onions, and the soothing silky texture of crema.

INGREDIENTS

3 poblano peppers

3 tablespoons extra virgin olive oil, plus more as needed

2 large Vidalia onions, halved and thinly sliced

Salt and black pepper, to taste

Kernels from 3 ears of corn

1 cup Mexican crema

¾ cup Manchego cheese, grated

Water or milk, as needed

1 Preheat the oven to 450°F. Place the poblanos on a parchment–lined baking sheet and place it on the center rack of the oven. Bake, while turning the peppers 3 to 4 times to promote even roasting, until the skins are completely wrinkled and charred, about 25 to 30 minutes. Remove from the oven, transfer the peppers to a mixing bowl, and cover with a kitchen towel. When they are cool enough to handle, remove the skin, seeds, and stems and cut into quarters.

2 Heat a large, deep skillet over low heat for 2 to 3 minutes. Add 3 tablespoons of the olive oil and heat for a couple of minutes. Raise the heat to medium–low, add the onions and a couple pinches of salt, and cook until the onions are brown and very soft, about 45 minutes, while stirring occasionally. Transfer ½ cup of the cooked onions to a small bowl and set aside.

3 Add the corn and a couple pinches of salt to the onions remaining in the skillet. If the pan looks really dry, add another tablespoon of olive oil. Increase the heat to medium, and cook until the corn starts to brown, about 10 minutes. Transfer the mixture to the bowl containing the onions.

4 While the corn is cooking, put the poblanos, the reserved caramelized onions, Mexican crema, Manchego, and 3 to 4 pinches of salt in a food processor or blender and puree until smooth. Add 1 to 2 tablespoons of water or milk if the mixture seems too thick.

5 Reheat the skillet over medium–low heat. Add more olive oil and heat for 1 or 2 minutes. Add the poblano puree, stir in the corn-and-onion mixture, and cook until heated through.

Salsa Verde

YIELD: 1 CUP • ACTIVE TIME: 15 MINUTES
TOTAL TIME: 30 MINUTES

Tangy tomatillos make this a lovely diversion from standard salsa.

1 Place the tomatillos and serrano peppers in a large saucepan and cover with water. Bring to a boil and cook until the tomatillos start to lose their bright green color, about 10 minutes.

2 Drain the water and transfer to a blender. Add the remaining ingredients and puree until smooth. Top with the cilantro and serve.

INGREDIENTS

10 tomatillos, husks removed, rinsed

8 to 10 serrano peppers, rinsed and stemmed

½ white onion

2 garlic cloves, minced

Kosher salt, to taste

¼ cup vegetable oil

1 bunch of cilantro, chopped, for garnish

Korean BBQ Sauce

YIELD: 3 CUPS • ACTIVE TIME: 15 MINUTES
TOTAL TIME: 35 MINUTES

Seek out another sauce if you aren't able to find gochujang, as there is no substitute for its flavor.

1 Place a small saucepan over medium heat.

2 Add the soy sauce, ketchup, rice wine vinegar, light brown sugar, gochujang, and garlic to the saucepan and stir until thoroughly combined. Bring to a simmer, cover the saucepan, and let simmer for 15 to 20 minutes, until the sauce has reduced by half.

3 Stir in the remaining ingredients, cook for 2 more minutes, and remove from heat.

4 Let the sauce stand for 10 minutes before serving.

INGREDIENTS

½ cup soy sauce

¼ cup ketchup

¼ cup rice wine vinegar

3 tablespoons light brown sugar

1 teaspoon gochujang (red chili paste)

2 garlic cloves, minced

1 teaspoon sesame oil

1 teaspoon ginger, grated

4 scallions, chopped

1 teaspoon coarsely ground black pepper

Kansas City BBQ Sauce

**YIELD: 5 CUPS • ACTIVE TIME: 10 MINUTES
TOTAL TIME: 40 MINUTES**

BBQ is a major source of regional pride, and this sauce makes it easy to understand why the folks in Kansas City believe their version to be the best.

INGREDIENTS

2 tablespoons olive oil

4 garlic cloves, minced

2 cups ketchup

1 cup water

¼ cup molasses

¼ cup dark brown sugar

¼ cup apple cider vinegar

2 tablespoons Worcestershire sauce

1 bay leaf

1 teaspoon mustard powder

1 teaspoon chili powder

1 teaspoon onion powder

2 teaspoons liquid smoke

1 teaspoon black pepper

1 teaspoon sea salt

1 Heat the olive oil in a saucepan over medium heat. Add the minced garlic cloves and cook until golden, about 2 minutes.

2 Stir the remaining ingredients into the saucepan and bring to a simmer. Cover the saucepan and cook until the sauce has been reduced by half, roughly 25 minutes. Make sure to stir the sauce occasionally.

3 When the sauce has been reduced by half, remove from heat, discard bay leaf, and let stand for 10 minutes before serving.

Variation: For additional kick, try adding half of a minced habanero pepper. Be careful, though, the more seeds you add the hotter the sauce will become.

Rose Sauce

**YIELD: 4 SERVINGS • ACTIVE TIME: 15 MINUTES
TOTAL TIME: 30 MINUTES**

Thick, creamy, and comforting, this sauce has never met a child it couldn't mesmerize. Reducing the cream is essential to this recipe, as it adds an even greater level of flavor and richness to the sauce.

1 Place the tomatoes in a food processor or blender and puree until smooth.

2 Heat a medium saucepan over medium–low heat for 2 to 3 minutes. Add the butter and raise the heat to medium. Once it melts and stops foaming, add the onion and a pinch of salt and stir. When it begins to gently sizzle, adjust the heat to low, cover, and cook, while stirring occasionally, until the onion has softened, about 10 minutes.

3 Add the pureed tomatoes and a couple pinches of salt. If the tomatoes are not in season, add the sugar and stir. Bring to a boil, then reduce the heat to low and simmer for 20 minutes. Remove the onion pieces with a slotted spoon.

4 As the tomato sauce cooks, add the cream to a small saucepan and cook over low heat until it has reduced by about half and then remove from heat. Once the tomato sauce has thickened, add the reduced cream, season with salt, and stir.

INGREDIENTS

4 pounds very ripe plum tomatoes, concasse (see page 128) and chopped

4 tablespoons unsalted butter

½ white or Vidalia onion, chopped

Salt, to taste

1 teaspoon sugar (optional)

2 cups heavy cream

Béchamel Sauce

YIELD: 4 TO 6 SERVINGS • ACTIVE TIME: 5 MINUTES
TOTAL TIME: 15 MINUTES

Which country is responsible for the existence of this sauce has long been a topic of debate between Italy and France, but we're certain about this: when properly prepared, béchamel adds a creamy texture and a light, buttery taste to any preparation.

INGREDIENTS

8 tablespoons (1 stick) unsalted butter

½ cup all–purpose flour

4 cups whole milk

½ teaspoon nutmeg, grated

Salt and freshly ground white pepper, to taste

1 Melt the butter in a medium saucepan over medium heat, making sure it does not brown. Add the flour all at once and quickly whisk until the mixture becomes velvety smooth. Cook, while whisking constantly, for 5 minutes, until the mixture stops foaming and turns golden.

2 Pour in ½ cup of the milk and whisk vigorously until you've loosened the mixture. Add the rest of the milk and cook, while whisking constantly. Within minutes the mixture will start to thicken. Add the nutmeg and season with salt and pepper. Stir to combine and use immediately or let cool, cover, and refrigerate for up to 2 days. Bring back to room temperature before using.

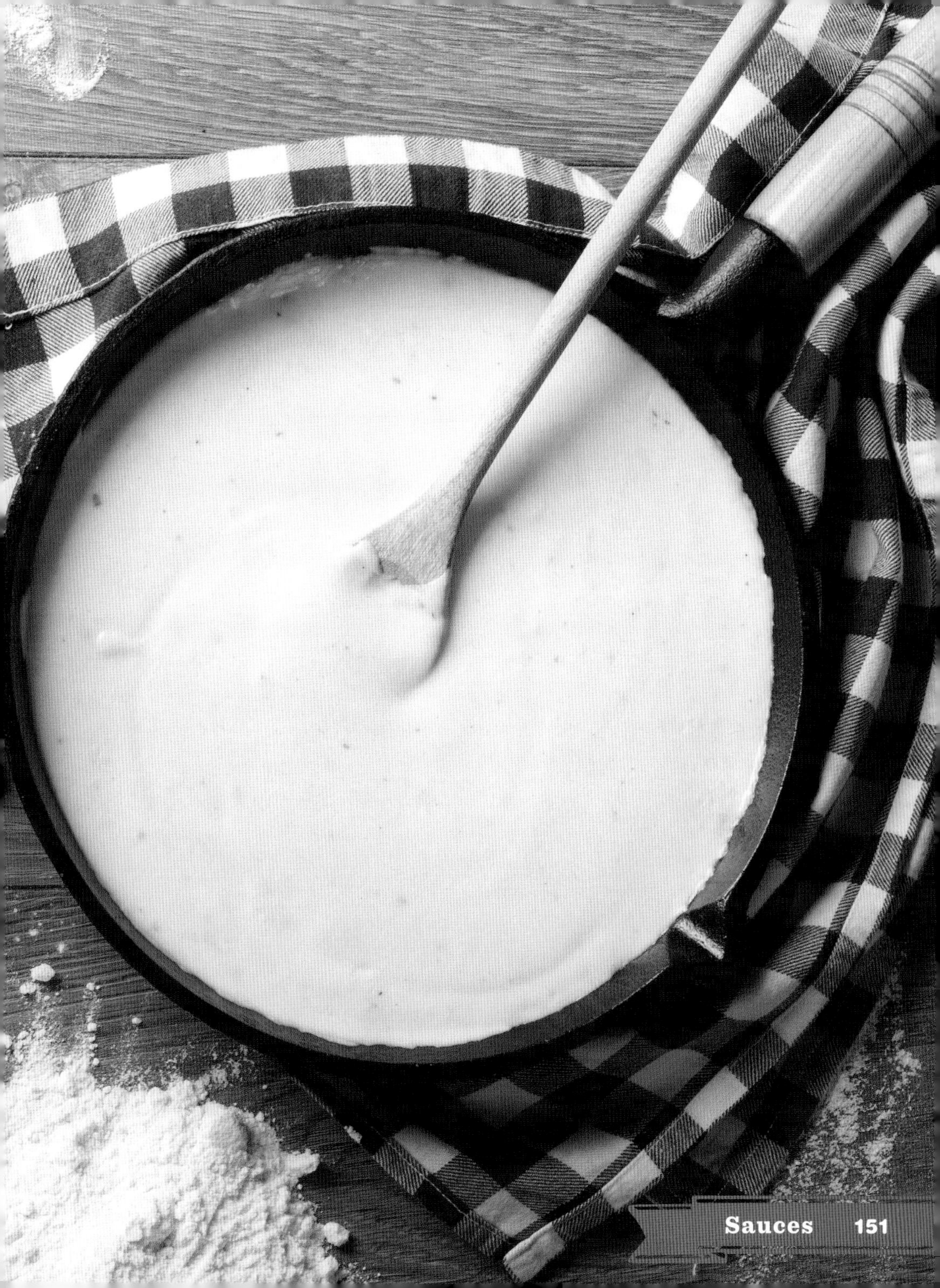

Peanut Sauce

YIELD: 1 CUP • ACTIVE TIME: 5 MINUTES
TOTAL TIME: 5 MINUTES

When you're looking to spruce up a flatbread filled with grilled chicken or veggies, turn to this sauce. This would also be great in place of the tomato sauce on the Bok Choy, Pine Nut, and Raisin Pizza (see page 73).

1 Place the peanut butter, water, soy sauce, and rice vinegar in a bowl and whisk until thoroughly combined.

2 Add the ginger, honey, and chili–garlic sauce and stir to combine.

INGREDIENTS

6 tablespoons natural peanut butter

6 tablespoons water (100°F to 105°F)

4 tablespoons soy sauce

1 tablespoon rice vinegar

1 tablespoon ginger, grated

2 teaspoons honey

1 teaspoon chili–garlic sauce

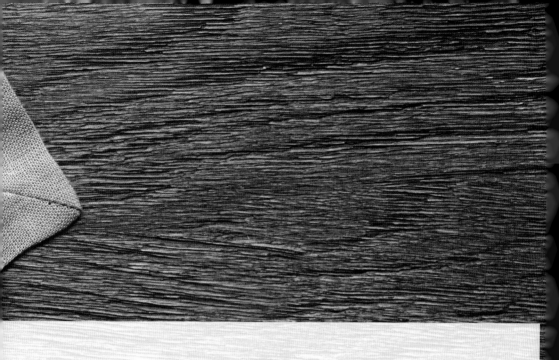

Toppings

Pizzas and flatbreads are adored because they can meet every request, accommodate all tastes, and utilize surplus ingredients that would otherwise go bad. They are a catchall without ever seeming like a last resort.

This chapter contains a number of toppings that you can whip up out of things that are probably kicking around in your pantry or refrigerator. So don't worry if one of your particularly picky friends drops in around dinnertime some night—you'll be able to find something in here that will wow them.

Apricot and Chili Jam

YIELD: 2 CUPS • ACTIVE TIME: 20 MINUTES
TOTAL TIME: 1½ HOURS

This spicy jam would be lovely on a pita filled with grilled chicken, or with some goat cheese on a Tunnbröd (see page 117).

INGREDIENTS

½ pound apricots

Zest and juice of ¼ small lemon

¼ pound white sugar

¼ cup water

1 red chili, prepared according to taste

1 teaspoon butter

1 Wash and dry all of the apricots. Cut in half and remove the stones from the center. Slice the fruit into smaller pieces and add to a large saucepan. Add the lemon zest and juice, the sugar, and the water.

2 Finely chop the chili. If desired, you can blend it in a food processor instead. Add the chili and the seeds to the saucepan and mix with the apricots. Slowly bring the mixture to a boil.

3 Stir gently until all of the sugar has dissolved. Allow the mixture to hold a rapid boil for a few minutes.

4 Reduce the heat to a simmer and cook for 15 to 20 minutes, stirring constantly to prevent the mixture from burning. If you prefer a chunkier jam, make sure to stir gently so that the chunks of fruit stay intact. If you want a smoother jam, mash the mixture as you stir.

5 To test your jam, remove a spoonful and drop it onto a chilled saucer. If a skin doesn't begin to form after a minute, continue simmering and testing.

6 If the jam feels like a soft jelly and has started to form a thin skin, remove the pan from the heat. Add the butter and stir to disperse any froth. Cool for 15 minutes, then fill your sterilized jam jar. Allow to cool completely before storing in the refrigerator.

Fig Jam

A Piadina (see page 122) filled with this, some Camembert, and a few slices of prosciutto would be absolute heaven.

INGREDIENTS

2 pounds figs, stemmed and cut into ½–inch pieces

1½ cups granulated sugar

¼ cup water

¼ cup lemon juice

Pinch of salt

1 vanilla bean, split and seeded (optional)

1 cinnamon stick (optional)

1 Place all of the ingredients in a medium saucepan and bring to a boil. Stir occasionally until the sugar is dissolved. If you include the vanilla bean in your preparation, add both the seeds and the pod.

2 Reduce heat to low. Cook, while stirring occasionally, for 30 minutes to 1 hour, or until the liquid is thick, sticky, and falls heavily from a spoon.

3 Remove pan from heat and, if using, discard the vanilla pod and the cinnamon stick.

4 For a chunky jam, gently mash the large pieces of fig with a fork or potato masher. For a smoother jam, puree the mixture in a food processor.

5 Spoon the jam into sterilized jars, leaving ¹/₄–inch space at the top and cover with lids. Let cool to room temperature, then refrigerate. Store the jam in the refrigerator for up to 2 months.

Cilantro–Mint Chutney

YIELD: 2 CUPS • ACTIVE TIME: 5 MINUTES
TOTAL TIME: 5 MINUTES

If you are preparing some Naan (see page 109) to put alongside an Indian dish, you won't regret throwing this chutney on the table.

INGREDIENTS

2 cups fresh cilantro, packed

1 cup fresh mint leaves, packed

½ cup white onion, chopped

⅓ cup water

1 tablespoon fresh lime juice

1 teaspoon green chili, chopped (serrano or Thai are good options; include the seeds or adjust to your taste)

1 teaspoon sugar

¾ teaspoon salt, or to taste

Place all ingredients in a blender and puree. Take care not to over–puree the mixture. You want the chutney to have some texture.

Mostarda

YIELD: ½ CUP • ACTIVE TIME: 5 MINUTES
TOTAL TIME: 15 MINUTES

This condiment, which is perfect alongside any cured meat, hails from Northern Italy.

1 In a small saucepan, combine the apricots, cherries, shallot, ginger, wine, vinegar, water, and sugar and bring to a boil. Cover and cook over medium heat until all of the liquid has been absorbed and the fruit is soft, about 10 minutes.

2 Stir in the dried mustard, Dijon mustard, and butter. Simmer until the mixture is jam–like, about 2 to 3 minutes.

3 Serve warm or at room temperature, or store in the refrigerator for up to 1 week.

INGREDIENTS

¼ pound dried apricots, roughly chopped

¼ cup dried cherries, roughly chopped

1 shallot, minced

1½ teaspoons crystallized ginger, minced

½ cup dry white wine

3 tablespoons white wine vinegar

3 tablespoons water

3 tablespoons sugar

1 teaspoon dried mustard

1 teaspoon Dijon mustard

1 tablespoon unsalted butter

Olive Tapenade

YIELD: 1½ CUPS • ACTIVE TIME: 5 MINUTES
TOTAL TIME: 5 MINUTES

This spread can be made with any type of olives, but black olives produce the most aesthetically pleasing iteration.

INGREDIENTS

1½ cups pitted, brine–cured olives

1 teaspoon anchovy paste or 2 anchovy fillets, minced

3 tablespoons capers, rinsed

1½ tablespoons parsley, chopped

3 garlic cloves

3 tablespoons fresh lemon juice

¼ teaspoon black pepper, plus more to taste

¼ cup olive oil

Salt, to taste

1 In a food processor, combine the olives, anchovy component, capers, parsley, garlic, lemon juice, and black pepper. Pulse 2 to 3 times until coarsely chopped.

2 Drizzle in the olive oil and pulse a few more times until a chunky paste forms, scraping down the sides as needed.

3 Season to taste with salt and pepper and serve at room temperature.

Sun-Dried Tomato and Pistachio Tapenade

**YIELD: 1½ TO 2 CUPS • ACTIVE TIME: 10 MINUTES
TOTAL TIME: 20 MINUTES**

A few dollops of this would be positively delicious on veggie tacos, but it could also work as a pizza sauce.

1 Place the 1 tablespoon of olive oil in a nonstick sauté pan and warm over medium heat. Add the shallot and cook until light brown, about 3 to 5 minutes.

2 Deglaze the pan with vermouth. Remove from heat and let cool.

3 Place the contents of the pan and the remaining ingredients into a food processor and puree until well combined. If too thick, add water 1 teaspoon at a time until the desired consistency is achieved.

INGREDIENTS

¼ cup extra virgin olive oil, plus 1 tablespoon

1 shallot, minced

1 teaspoon dry vermouth

¾ cup sun-dried tomatoes packed in oil

½ cup pistachios, shelled

½ cup Italian parsley, chopped

1 teaspoon fresh thyme, minced

Zest and juice from ½ lemon

1 teaspoon sea salt

1 teaspoon freshly ground black pepper

Water, as needed

Hummus

There's no need to rely on the store to get your fix of Middle Eastern flavors. Once you spread this on a homemade pita (see page 105), you'll never go back.

INGREDIENTS

1 (15 oz.) can of chickpeas

3 tablespoons extra virgin olive oil

3 tablespoons tahini

1½ tablespoons lemon juice, plus more as needed

1 small garlic clove, roughly chopped

1 teaspoon salt

½ teaspoon finely ground black pepper

1 Drain the chickpeas into a strainer, reserving the liquid from the can. If time allows, remove the skins from each of the chickpeas. This will make your hummus much smoother.

2 Place the chickpeas, olive oil, tahini, lemon juice, garlic, salt, and pepper in a food processor.

3 Puree the hummus until it is very smooth, about 5 to 10 minutes. Scrape down the sides of the bowl as needed to integrate any large chunks.

4 Taste and adjust the seasoning. If your hummus is stiffer than you'd like, add 2 to 3 tablespoons of the reserved chickpea liquid and blend until desired consistency is achieved.

Variation: For even tastier and more authentic hummus, soak dried chickpeas overnight and cook them for 1 hour.

Chickpea Carrot Salad

YIELD: 6 SERVINGS • ACTIVE TIME: 15 MINUTES
TOTAL TIME: 45 MINUTES

Pair this simple salad with some tortillas or pitas and you've got a dinner that's delicious and nutritious.

1 Combine chickpeas, carrots, celery, scallions, dill, and toasted pumpkin seeds in a medium bowl and set aside.

2 Combine the olive oil, vinegar, garlic, salt, and pepper in a small bowl. Whisk together until well combined and pour over the chickpea–and–carrot mixture. Stir well to combine.

3 Allow the salad to chill in the refrigerator for 30 minutes before serving.

INGREDIENTS

2 (15 oz.) cans of chickpeas, rinsed and drained

2 cups carrots, peeled and chopped

⅔ cup celery, chopped

½ cup scallions, sliced thin

½ cup dill, chopped

½ cup toasted pumpkin seeds, chopped

⅓ cup extra virgin olive oil

2 to 3 tablespoons sherry vinegar

1 large garlic clove, minced

¼ teaspoon salt

Coarsely ground black pepper, to taste

Roasted Artichoke and Garlic Spread

YIELD: 1 CUP • ACTIVE TIME: 5 MINUTES
TOTAL TIME: 10 TO 20 MINUTES

Pairing the nutty flavor of artichokes with the sweetness of roasted garlic makes for an incredibly versatile spread. This is also worth trying out on a pizza.

INGREDIENTS

1 (12 oz.) bag of frozen artichoke hearts, thawed and halved or quartered

4 garlic cloves, peeled

2 tablespoons white vinegar or apple cider vinegar

¼ teaspoon salt

4 tablespoons olive oil

Pinch of onion powder (optional)

1 Spread the artichoke hearts and garlic on a cookie sheet and broil for 5 to 15 minutes, until browned.

2 Combine the artichokes, garlic, and remaining ingredients in a blender or food processor and puree until desired texture is achieved.

Grilled Corn Guacamole

YIELD: 1½ CUPS • ACTIVE TIME: 10 MINUTES
TOTAL TIME: 15 MINUTES

This guacamole utilizes grilled corn to add some extra sweetness and is good enough to eat with a spoon.

1 Preheat your gas or charcoal grill to medium–high heat.

2 When the grill is 450°F, place the corn on the grill and cook, while turning occasionally, until all sides are charred. This should take about 8 minutes. Remove from the grill and let cool. When cool enough to handle, remove the kernels from the cob and set aside.

3 Place the avocados in a medium bowl. Using a fork, mash the avocado until it reaches the desired consistency. Add corn, cilantro, onion, serrano peppers, lime juice, and feta. Stir until the mixture is the desired consistency and season with salt and pepper.

INGREDIENTS

1 ear of corn, shucked

Meat from 3 avocados

¼ cup cilantro, chopped

¼ cup red onion, diced

2 serrano peppers, seeded and minced

2 tablespoons lime juice

¼ cup feta cheese

Salt and pepper, to taste

Lentil–Avocado Dip

YIELD: 1½ CUPS • ACTIVE TIME: 5 MINUTES
TOTAL TIME: 1 HOUR AND 40 MINUTES

Per usual, avocados make everything better.

INGREDIENTS

2 cups water

1 cup dried lentils

Meat from 1 avocado

1 tablespoon tahini

Juice of 2 limes

½ cup extra virgin olive oil

2 teaspoons sea salt

2 teaspoons freshly ground black pepper

1 teaspoon coriander

3 dashes of Tabasco

1 Bring the water to boil in a medium saucepan and add the lentils. Turn heat to low and let simmer until lentils are cooked through and all the water is absorbed, 20 to 30 minutes. Remove from heat and let cool.

2 Add the lentils and the remaining ingredients to a food processor and puree until smooth. Let chill in refrigerator for 1 to 2 hours and serve.

Herb–Marinated Goat Cheese

YIELD: 1 CUP • ACTIVE TIME: 10 MINUTES
TOTAL TIME: 1 HOUR AND 10 MINUTES

A selection of fresh seasonal herbs soaked in olive oil infuse the goat cheese with deliciously vibrant flavors, while still allowing the cheese's tanginess to shine through.

1 Slice the goat cheese into thick rounds.

2 Gently roll cheese rounds in the herbs and press so that the herbs adhere to the surface of the cheese.

3 Layer the goat cheese rounds in glass jars. Pour olive oil over the cheese until it's almost covered.

4 Let marinate for 1 hour. The cheese can be stored for up to a week in the fridge.

Tip: You can include roasted garlic cloves or a pinch of red pepper flakes to boost the flavor.

INGREDIENTS

8 oz. fresh goat cheese

⅓ cup fresh herbs, chopped (tarragon, chives, and thyme are recommended)

1 cup extra virgin olive oil

Smoked Sweet Onions

YIELD: 4 SERVINGS • ACTIVE TIME: 15 MINUTES
TOTAL TIME: 1 HOUR AND 45 MINUTES

Cutting the natural sweetness of the onions with a bit of smoke from the grill makes these a perfect pizza topping. Give them a try on the Chorizo and Olive Pizza (see page 37) or the Deep Dish Bacon Pizza (see page 38).

INGREDIENTS

2 to 3 cups hickory wood chips

4 large sweet onions, quartered

4 garlic cloves, minced

¼ cup butter, cut into small pieces

1 teaspoon salt

1 Soak the wood chips in a bowl of water 1 hour before you are ready to grill.

2 Preheat your gas or charcoal grill to medium heat.

3 Place the onions in a large piece of foil. Sprinkle the minced garlic over them and dot with the pieces of butter.

4 Add the salt, fold the foil over, and crimp the edges to form a foil packet.

5 When the grill is about 400°F, scatter the wood chips over the coals or place them in a smoker box. Place the packet on the grill and cook for 20 minutes. Remove the onions from the packet, place directly on the grill, and cook until lightly charred, about 3 to 4 minutes.

Grilled Peach Salad

YIELD: 4 SERVINGS • ACTIVE TIME: 5 MINUTES
TOTAL TIME: 20 MINUTES

Add a little bit of goat cheese and this salad will go a long way on any of the flatbreads in this book.

1 Preheat your gas or charcoal grill to high heat.

2 When the grill is 500°F, brush the cut side of each peach with half of the olive oil and place directly on the grill, cut side down. Brush the bell pepper slices with the remaining oil and place them on the grill as well.

3 Grill the peaches for 2 to 3 minutes, or until they become caramelized. Flip them over, cook for 2 minutes to heat through, and transfer them to a cutting board. Grill the bell peppers for about 8 minutes, turning over once. Remove from the grill and transfer to the cutting board. Chop the peaches and peppers into bite–sized pieces.

4 In a large bowl, combine the peaches, peppers, arugula, and slivered almonds and toss. Drizzle honey and lemon juice over the top, toss to coat, and serve.

INGREDIENTS

3 peaches,
pitted and halved

2 tablespoons olive oil

2 bell peppers, sliced

4 cups arugula

3 tablespoons
slivered almonds

1 tablespoon honey

½ tablespoon
lemon juice

Grilled Zucchini Salad

YIELD: 4 SERVINGS • ACTIVE TIME: 5 MINUTES
TOTAL TIME: 20 MINUTES

There are a number of uses for this salad, but we think it works best as the filling for a quesadilla.

INGREDIENTS

2 zucchini, cut into strips

1 red bell pepper, cut into strips

1 yellow squash, cut into strips

1 tablespoon olive oil, plus ½ teaspoon

Salt and pepper, to taste

1 (15 oz.) can of white beans

1 garlic clove, minced

1 cup baby spinach

1 Preheat your gas or charcoal grill to medium heat. In a large bowl, add the zucchini, bell pepper, squash, and the 1 tablespoon of olive oil. Season with salt and pepper and toss to coat.

2 When the grill is 400°F, place the zucchini, bell pepper, and squash on the grill and cook for 4 to 6 minutes per side, flipping over once. Remove from grill, transfer to a cutting board, and slice thin.

3 In a medium bowl, combine the beans, garlic, and remaining olive oil. Mash together until the mixture becomes smooth. Add the spinach and grilled vegetables, stir to combine, and season with salt and pepper.

Grilled Zucchini Parmesan

YIELD: 4 SERVINGS • ACTIVE TIME: 15 MINUTES
TOTAL TIME: 20 MINUTES

There's never a shortage of zucchini in the summer, and this is another inventive way to make use of the bounty.

1 Preheat your gas or charcoal grill to medium–high heat.

2 In a small bowl, mix together the zucchini, olive oil, butter, garlic, and parsley. Season with salt and toss to coat.

3 When the grill is 450°F, place the zucchini on the grill and cook until the slices are tender, about 8 minutes.

4 Remove the zucchini from the grill and sprinkle one side with the Parmesan. Spread the tomato sauce on top and serve.

INGREDIENTS

3 zucchini, halved lengthwise

2 tablespoons olive oil

2 tablespoons butter, softened

2 garlic cloves, minced

1 tablespoon parsley, chopped

Salt, to taste

½ cup Parmesan cheese, grated

¼ cup tomato sauce, homemade (see page 129) or store–bought

Grilled Plums with Balsamic Glaze

YIELD: 4 SERVINGS • ACTIVE TIME: 10 MINUTES
TOTAL TIME: 25 MINUTES

Grilled plums are a cookout classic, but the sweet and tangy balsamic glaze takes them up another notch. This preparation and some prosciutto would be lovely on a pizza.

INGREDIENTS

1 cup balsamic vinegar

2 teaspoons lemon zest

4 firm plums, halved

1 Preheat your gas or charcoal grill to medium heat. Place the balsamic vinegar and lemon zest in a small saucepan and bring to a boil. Cook until the mixture becomes syrupy, 10 to 12 minutes.

2 When the grill is 400°F, place the plums on the grill and cook for 4 to 6 minutes, flipping them over halfway. Once the plums are tender, remove and let cool.

3 When the plums are cool enough to handle, cut them into bite–sized cubes. Place them in a bowl, drizzle with the balsamic glaze, and stir to coat.

Roasted Cherry Tomatoes

YIELD: 4 SERVINGS • ACTIVE TIME: 25 MINUTES
TOTAL TIME: 25 MINUTES

Thanks to the addition of rosemary, these tomatoes are sweet and savory enough to fit in almost anywhere.

1 Preheat your oven to 450°F. Place the cherry tomatoes in a bowl with the oil, garlic, salt, and pepper. Toss to coat and transfer to a baking dish.

2 Roast the tomatoes in the oven for 10 minutes. Remove from the oven, stir the tomatoes around to ensure even roasting, and return to the oven. Roast for another 5 minutes, remove, stir, and sprinkle with the rosemary. Return to the oven and cook for another 5 minutes, until the tomatoes are charred.

3 Season with additional salt and pepper and serve.

INGREDIENTS

1 pint cherry tomatoes

1 tablespoon olive oil

1 garlic clove, minced

½ teaspoon salt, plus more to taste

Black pepper, to taste

2 teaspoons fresh rosemary

Sautéed Greens

**YIELD: 4 TO 6 SERVINGS • ACTIVE TIME: 20 MINUTES
TOTAL TIME: 30 MINUTES**

These cooked greens are a lovely base for a health–conscious flatbread. They will work wonderfully with the Chickpea Carrot Salad (see page 173).

INGREDIENTS

2 tablespoons olive oil, plus more as needed

2 garlic cloves, sliced thin

½ teaspoon red pepper flakes

1 bunch of Swiss chard, tough ends removed, leaves chopped,

1 bunch of kale, tough stems removed, leaves chopped

Salt and pepper, to taste

1 Place the oil in a cast–iron skillet and warm over medium–high heat. Add the garlic and cook until garlic begins to bounce, about 1 to 2 minutes.

2 Add the red pepper flakes and greens and gently stir. Reduce the heat to medium and continue to stir as the greens cook down.

3 Once cooked down, allow the greens to cook over medium heat, while stirring occasionally, until wilted and tender, about 5 to 10 minutes. If necessary, add more oil to the pan while cooking.

4 When the greens are soft and tender, transfer to a bowl, season with salt and pepper, and serve.

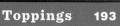

Eggplant Parm

**YIELD: 4 SERVINGS • ACTIVE TIME: 20 MINUTES
TOTAL TIME: 1½ HOURS**

Rich with garlic, fresh mozzarella, and Parmesan cheese—this eggplant dish is almost a pizza in its own right. Toss it on a Schuttelbrot (see page 121) to counter the gooey texture with some crunch.

1 Preheat the oven to 350°F. Put the slices of eggplant in a single layer on paper towels, sprinkle salt over them, and let rest for about 15 minutes. Turn the slices over, sprinkle with salt, and let sit for another 15 minutes.

2 Rinse the eggplant and dry with paper towels.

3 Drizzle the oil over a baking sheet. In a shallow bowl, combine the bread crumbs and Parmesan cheese. Put the beaten egg in another shallow bowl. Dip the slices of eggplant in the egg, then the bread crumb mixture, coating both sides. Transfer the eggplant to a baking sheet.

4 Bake in the oven for about 10 minutes, turn them over, and bake for another 10 minutes. Remove the sheet from the oven and set aside.

5 Put a layer of tomato sauce in a baking dish and stir in the garlic. Lay the eggplant slices in the sauce, layering to fit. Top with the shredded mozzarella.

6 Put the dish in the oven and bake for about 30 minutes, until the sauce is bubbling and the cheese is golden brown. Remove, let cool for about 10 minutes, and serve.

INGREDIENTS

- 1 large eggplant, cut into ¼–inch slices
- Salt, to taste
- 2 tablespoons olive oil
- 1 cup Italian bread crumbs
- 2 tablespoons Parmesan cheese, grated
- 1 egg, beaten
- ½ cup tomato sauce, homemade (see page 129) or store–bought
- 2 garlic cloves, minced
- 8 oz. mozzarella cheese, shredded

Thai Tofu and Eggplant

YIELD: 4 SERVINGS • ACTIVE TIME: 15 MINUTES
TOTAL TIME: 40 MINUTES

With such unique and amazing flavors, you really can't go wrong, but we recommend serving this on top of the Roti (see page 114).

INGREDIENTS

1 large eggplant, sliced

Salt, to taste

2 tablespoons olive oil

3 red bell peppers, sliced

4 garlic cloves, minced

1 small onion, quartered

3 teaspoons brown sugar

2 tablespoons lime juice

8 oz. tofu, drained and diced

1 teaspoon soy sauce

¼ cup basil leaves

1 Put the slices of eggplant in a single layer on paper towels, sprinkle salt over them, and let rest for about 15 minutes. Turn the slices over, sprinkle with salt, and let sit for another 15 minutes. Rinse the eggplant and dry with paper towels.

2 Place the olive oil in a skillet and warm over medium heat. Place the eggplant in the skillet and cook, while stirring, for 8 to 10 minutes, until the eggplant is tender. Remove from the skillet and let cool.

3 Place the red peppers, garlic, onion, sugar, and lime juice in a food processor or blender and puree until smooth.

4 Place the red pepper puree in the skillet and cook over medium heat for 1 minute.

5 Drizzle the soy sauce over the tofu. Add the tofu, eggplant, and half of the basil to the skillet. Cook until they are sufficiently heated through.

6 Remove and garnish with the remaining basil.

Lemon–Garlic Mushrooms

YIELD: 4 SERVINGS • ACTIVE TIME: 10 MINUTES
TOTAL TIME: 25 MINUTES

The three wonderful flavors in this dish would be lovely when paired with the Sautéed Greens (see page 192).

1 Cook brown rice according to the instructions on the package and set aside.

2 In a small bowl, combine the garlic, parsley, half of the olive oil, lemon juice, and ginger. Season with pepper, add the mushrooms, and toss to coat. Set aside.

3 Place the remaining olive oil in a skillet and warm over medium–high heat. Add the mushroom mixture and cook until the mushrooms begin to release their moisture, about 5 minutes. Reduce the heat to medium and cook for 10 minutes.

4 Transfer the mushrooms to a large bowl. Add the brown rice and toss to coat.

INGREDIENTS

1 cup brown rice

3 garlic cloves, minced

3 tablespoons parsley, minced

4 tablespoons olive oil

2 tablespoons lemon juice

2 tablespoons ginger, grated

Black pepper, to taste

1 pound mushrooms, diced

Ceviche

**YIELD: 6 TO 8 SERVINGS • ACTIVE TIME: 10 MINUTES
TOTAL TIME: 20 TO 30 MINUTES**

A lovely, fresh filling when you're looking to take your tacos in a slightly different direction.

INGREDIENTS

1 pound shrimp, peeled and deveined

Juice of 5 limes

2 shallots, minced

½ English cucumber, diced

1 cup cilantro, chopped

2 teaspoons sea salt

2 teaspoons freshly ground black pepper

Place the ingredients in a bowl, toss to combine, place in the refrigerator, and let chill for 10 to 20 minutes.

Variation: Substitute fresh salmon, tuna, fluke, red snapper, or lobster for the shrimp. Diced avocado makes for a lovely addition.

Curried Chicken Salad

Madras curry powder provides a nice layer of flavor that goes well with the tart Granny Smith apples and the rich pecans.

1 Preheat the oven to 350°F. Place the chicken on a baking sheet. Season with salt and pepper and drizzle with enough olive oil to coat. Place the chicken in the oven and bake for 30 minutes, or until the center of the chicken reaches 160°F. Remove from the oven and let rest for 10 minutes so that the chicken cools and retains its juices.

2 In a large salad bowl, combine the mayonnaise, lime juice, all of the spices, celery, apples, red pepper, and pecans.

3 Once the chicken has cooled, dice into small cubes and add to the bowl. Stir to combine and serve.

INGREDIENTS

1½ pounds boneless, skinless chicken breasts, cut into ½–inch thick cutlets

Salt and pepper, to taste

Dash of olive oil

1 cup mayonnaise

3 tablespoons fresh lime juice

¼ cup Madras curry powder

1 tablespoon cumin

1 tablespoon granulated garlic

½ teaspoon cinnamon

½ teaspoon turmeric

2 cups celery, minced

2 Granny Smith apples, minced

½ red bell pepper, seeded and minced

½ cup pecans

Coconut Curry Chicken

YIELD: 4 TO 6 SERVINGS • ACTIVE TIME: 20 MINUTES
TOTAL TIME: 1 HOUR

The creamy coconut milk tempers the spice enough just enough to ensure that your experience is pure pleasure.

INGREDIENTS

5 tablespoons green curry paste

4 to 6 boneless chicken thighs

2 yellow onions, peeled and sliced ¼-inch thick

2 red bell peppers, seeded and sliced ¼-inch thick

3 tablespoons ginger, peeled and mashed

1 garlic clove, peeled and mashed

3 tablespoons fish sauce

1 tablespoon Madras curry powder

¼ cup lite coconut milk

2 tablespoons Thai basil, chopped

1 Preheat oven to 375°F. Rub 2 tablespoons of the green curry paste on the chicken and set aside for at least 30 minutes.

2 Place a cast–iron skillet over medium–high heat and add the chicken thighs, skin side down. Cook until the skin is crispy, turn over, and cook for another 3 minutes. Remove the chicken from the skillet and set aside.

3 Add the onions, peppers, ginger, and garlic to the skillet and cook while stirring for 5 to 7 minutes. As the vegetables and aromatics are cooking, make sure you scrape the bottom of the pan to remove all of the browned bits on the bottom.

4 Add the remaining green curry paste and cook for an additional 3 minutes, until fragrant. Add the fish sauce, Madras curry powder, coconut milk, and Thai basil and stir until combined. Return the chicken to the pan and cook over low heat until heated through. As the coconut milk is just for flavor, you will want to use a slotted spoon to remove the chicken and vegetables from the skillet so that your flatbread doesn't get too soggy.

BBQ Chicken Hash

Got some leftover BBQ chicken? Whip this Southern-style hash up and top with sour cream.

1 Put the potatoes in a saucepan and cover with cold water. Add the 1 teaspoon of salt. Bring to a boil, then lower the heat and cook the potatoes for about 10 minutes. You don't want to cook them until they are tender, as this will cause them to fall apart in the hash. Drain, rinse with cold water, and set aside.

2 Heat the butter in a cast-iron skillet over medium-high heat. Add the onion, garlic, and slices of jalapeño, and cook, while stirring, until the vegetables soften, about 3 minutes.

3 Add the potatoes and press down into the skillet. Allow them to cook for about 5 minutes, then start turning sections over with a spatula while stirring in the chicken and the BBQ sauce. Continue to cook for about 5 minutes, until the potatoes are browned and the chicken is warmed through. Season with salt and pepper and top with sour cream.

INGREDIENTS

2 large russet potatoes, peeled and cubed

1 teaspoon salt, plus more to taste

3 tablespoons butter

1 Vidalia onion, diced

3 garlic cloves, minced

1 small jalapeño pepper, cored and seeded, sliced

1 pound cooked BBQ chicken, cut into bite-sized pieces

¼ cup BBQ sauce

Freshly ground pepper, to taste

Sour cream, for topping

Puerto Rican Rice and Beans

YIELD: 6 SERVINGS • ACTIVE TIME: 25 MINUTES
TOTAL TIME: 16 HOURS

Fill some Flour Tortillas (see page 88) with this gorgeous and authentic preparation and make burritos for a dinner that is sure to satisfy even the most ravenous of guests.

INGREDIENTS

1 cup kidney beans, soaked overnight and drained

½ cup vegetable oil

4 boneless, skinless chicken thighs

2 pieces of salt pork, minced (about ½ cup)

2 cups tomato sauce, homemade (see page 129) or store-bought

2 cups white rice

3 to 3½ cups chicken stock

2 packets Sazón with achiote

2 tablespoons dried oregano

1 cup Spanish olives with the brine

Adobo seasoning, to taste

---

1 Place the beans in a Dutch oven and cover with water. Bring to a boil, reduce heat to medium–low, and cover the pot. Cook for 45 minutes to 1 hour, until the beans are tender. Drain and set the beans aside.

2 Place the pot back on the stove and add ¼ cup of the oil. Add the chicken and cook over medium–high heat for 5 minutes on each side. Remove the chicken from the Dutch oven, cut it into 12 pieces, and set aside.

3 Add the salt pork and the remaining oil to the pot and cook until some of the salt pork's fat has rendered, about 5 minutes. Add the tomato sauce and cook for 5 minutes, while stirring constantly.

4 Add the rice to the pot, stir, and cook for 5 minutes.

5 Add the remaining ingredients and return the chicken to the pot. Reduce heat to medium and cook for 10 minutes. Cover the Dutch oven and cook for another 20 to 30 minutes, or until the liquid has been absorbed and the rice is tender.

6 Uncover the pot and add the beans. Stir to combine and serve.

Sausage and Peppers

**YIELD: 4 TO 6 SERVINGS • ACTIVE TIME: 40 MINUTES
TOTAL TIME: 1 HOUR**

This combination is a classic for a reason. If you sauté everything until it is crispy and caramelized, this preparation can work on a number of pizzas and flatbreads.

INGREDIENTS

4 tablespoons olive oil

1 pound sweet Italian sausage

4 garlic cloves, sliced thin

3 bell peppers, sliced thin

1 jalapeño pepper, seeded and sliced thin

1 large onion, sliced thin

Salt and pepper, to taste

1 Preheat oven to 350°F. Heat a cast–iron skillet over medium–high heat. Add 1 tablespoon of the olive oil and the sausages. Cook until the sausages are golden brown on all sides—about 3 minutes a side. Transfer the sausages to a plate and set aside.

2 Add the remaining oil, garlic, peppers, and onion. Cook, while stirring, until the vegetables soften, about 5 to 6 minutes. Return the sausages to the skillet.

3 Put the skillet in the oven and bake for about 15 minutes, until sausages are cooked through and the vegetables are tender and slightly crunchy on the outside. Season with salt and pepper and serve.

Kefta & Tzatziki

A pita filled with this savory, creamy dish is absolute heaven on a summer night.

1 Prepare the Tzatziki. Place all ingredients in a small bowl and whisk until the mixture is well combined. Transfer to the refrigerator until ready to serve.

2 Prepare the Kefta. In a mixing bowl, add all ingredients except for the olive oil and stir until well combined. Cook a small bit of the mixture as a test and taste. Adjust seasoning as necessary. Then form the mixture into 18 ovals. Place three meatballs on each skewer. Place the olive oil in a Dutch oven and warm over medium–high heat. Working in batches, add three skewers to the pot and sear the Kefta for 2 minutes on each side.

3 When all of the Kefta have been cooked, return all of the skewers to the pot, cover, and remove it from heat. Let stand for 10 minutes so the Kefta get cooked through. When they are cooked through, remove from the skewers and serve with the Tzatziki.

INGREDIENTS

For the Tzatziki
1 cup plain Greek yogurt
1 cucumber, seeded and grated
2 garlic cloves, minced
1 teaspoon lemon zest
1 tablespoon freshly squeezed lemon juice
2 tablespoons dill, chopped
Salt and black pepper, to taste

For the Kefta
1 pound ground beef (85% lean recommended)
1 pound ground lamb
½ cup white onion, minced
2 garlic cloves, roasted and mashed
Zest of 1 lemon
1 cup parsley, washed and minced
2 tablespoons mint, chopped
1 teaspoon cinnamon
2 tablespoons cumin
1 tablespoon paprika
1 teaspoon ground coriander
Salt and black pepper, to taste
¼ cup olive oil
6 wooden skewers

Desserts

Pizza and flatbreads are almost exclusively thought of as a savory preparation, but if we've learned anything through our love affair with them, it's to not try and box them in. It turns out, there is plenty of space for them to provide the sweet finish so many of us crave at the end of a day.

You may be skeptical, but after you try the Caramel Apple Pizza (see page 220) or the Chocolate Hazelnut and Strawberry Pizza (see page 228), we're pretty confident you'll start to see things our way.

Raspberry and Almond Paste Pizza

YIELD: 1 PIZZA • ACTIVE TIME: 10 MINUTES
TOTAL TIME: 25 MINUTES

Tuck the recipe for this delicious almond paste away, as it will come in handy in a number of other preparations.

INGREDIENTS

1 cup sliced almonds

½ cup unsalted butter, melted

5 tablespoons powdered sugar

1 egg yolk

½ teaspoon vanilla extract

1 ball of Basic Pizza Dough (see page 17), stretched into a 10–inch round

2 cups raspberries

1 Preheat your oven to 550°F. Place the almonds, butter, sugar, egg yolk, and vanilla into a food processor or blender and puree until it is a smooth fine paste.

2 Place the pizza dough in the oven and bake until golden brown, about 10 minutes. Remove from oven and let cool slightly.

3 Spread the almond paste on the cooked pizza crust, distribute the raspberries, and serve.

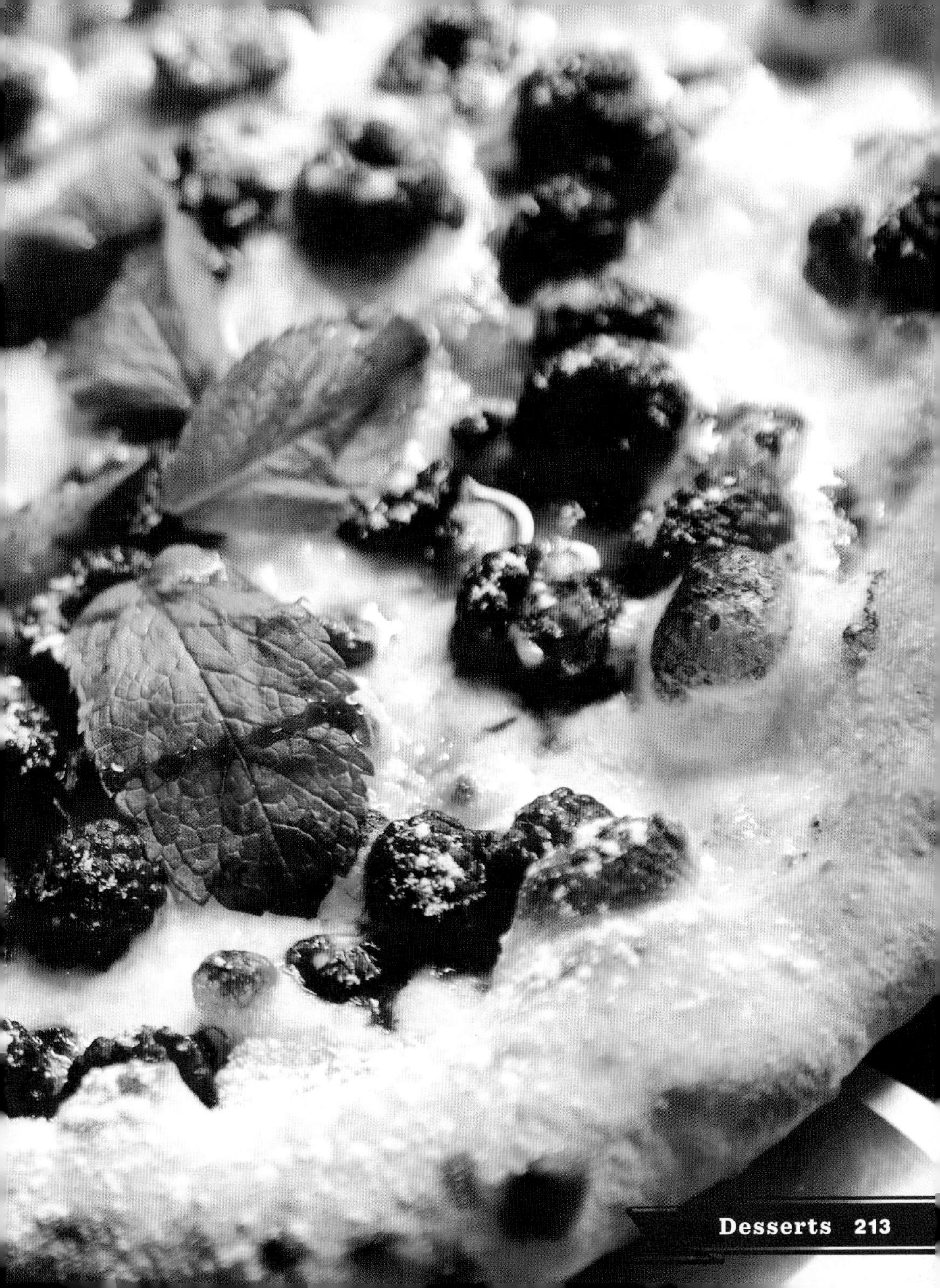

Vanilla Custard Pizza

YIELD: 1 PIZZA • ACTIVE TIME: 15 MINUTES
TOTAL TIME: 1 HOUR

After trying this twist on the classic pudding pie, you might just end up throwing out all of your pie plates.

1 Preheat your oven to 550°F. In a small bowl, whisk together the sugar and cornstarch. Add the eggs and whisk until smooth and creamy.

2 Place the milk and butter in a small saucepan and bring to a simmer over medium heat. Pour half of the hot milk–and–butter mixture into the egg mixture and stir until incorporated. Add the salt and vanilla extract and then pour this mixture into the saucepan. Cook, while stirring constantly, until the mixture is very thick and boiling. Remove from heat and pour the custard into a bowl. Place plastic wrap directly on top of the custard to prevent a skin from forming and transfer to the refrigerator until cool.

3 Place the pizza dough in the oven and bake until golden brown, about 10 minutes. Remove from oven and let cool slightly.

4 Spread custard on the cooked pizza crust, spread whipped cream on top, top with the chocolate shavings, and serve.

INGREDIENTS

½ cup sugar

3 tablespoons cornstarch

2 large eggs

2 cups milk

1 tablespoon butter

Pinch of salt

½ teaspoon vanilla extract

1 ball of Basic Pizza Dough (see page 17), stretched into a 10–inch round

Whipped cream, for topping

Chocolate shavings, for topping

Lemon Curd Pizza

YIELD: 1 PIZZA • ACTIVE TIME: 10 TO 15 MINUTES
TOTAL TIME: 40 TO 50 MINUTES

Placing the lemon curd topping under the broiler for a few minutes is the key to this dessert pizza, as it really brings out the sweetness.

INGREDIENTS

½ cup freshly squeezed lemon juice

2 teaspoons lemon zest

3 large eggs

⅔ cup sugar

8 tablespoons (1 stick) butter

1 ball of Basic Pizza Dough (see page 17), stretched into a 10-inch round

Whipped cream, for topping

1 Preheat the oven to 550°F. Place the lemon juice, lemon zest, eggs, sugar, and butter in a bowl and mix until well combined. Pour mixture into a saucepan and cook over low heat until it has thickened, approximately 10 minutes. Transfer to a bowl and chill in the refrigerator until it thickens further.

2 Place the pizza in the oven and bake until golden brown, about 10 minutes. Remove from oven and let cool slightly. Turn on the broiler.

3 Spread the lemon curd on the cooked pizza crust and place under the broiler for 2 minutes. Remove, top with whipped cream, and serve.

Tiramisu Pizza

YIELD: 1 PIZZA • ACTIVE TIME: 15 MINUTES
TOTAL TIME: 25 MINUTES

By transforming tiramisu into a spread, you're able to improve upon two Italian classics.

1 In a standing mixer, beat together the cheeses, sugar, vanilla, brewed espresso, espresso powder, and Kahlua until thoroughly combined.

2 Transfer to a bowl and dust with cocoa powder. Place in refrigerator until chilled.

3 Place the pizza in the oven and bake until golden brown, about 10 minutes. Remove from oven and let cool slightly.

4 Spread the tiramisu mixture over the cooked pizza crust, distribute the chocolate chips on top, and serve.

INGREDIENTS

1⅓ cups mascarpone cheese

½ cup fresh ricotta cheese

½ cup powdered sugar

1 teaspoon pure vanilla extract

2 tablespoons brewed espresso

1 teaspoon fine espresso powder

2 tablespoons Kahlua

1 teaspoon cocoa powder

1 ball of Basic Pizza Dough (see page 17), stretched into a 10-inch round

½ cup semi-sweet chocolate chips, chopped

Caramel Apple Pizza

YIELD: 6 TO 8 SERVINGS • ACTIVE TIME: 20 MINUTES
TOTAL TIME: 40 MINUTES

By combining a number of fall favorites into one dessert, you'll forget about the fast approach of winter.

INGREDIENTS

1 cup sugar

¼ cup water

3 tablespoons butter

½ teaspoon sea salt

1 ball of Basic Pizza Dough (see page 17), stretched into a 10–inch round

2 Granny Smith apples, sliced

2 tablespoons cinnamon

1 Preheat oven to 550°F. Place the sugar, water, butter, and salt in a small saucepan and cook over medium–high heat until the mixture is light brown. Be sure not to stir the mixture; instead, swirl the pan a few times.

2 Reduce heat to medium and cook for about 3 to 5 minutes, or until the mixture caramelizes. Stir the mixture once or twice to make sure it does not burn. Remove from heat and let cool slightly.

3 Place the pizza in the oven and cook until golden brown, about 10 minutes. Remove from oven and let cool slightly.

4 Place the apples in a baking dish and sprinkle with the cinnamon. Reduce the heat to 350°F and bake the apples until they are tender, about 15 minutes.

5 Place the baked apple slices on top of the cooked crust in an even layer and then drizzle the caramel over the top.

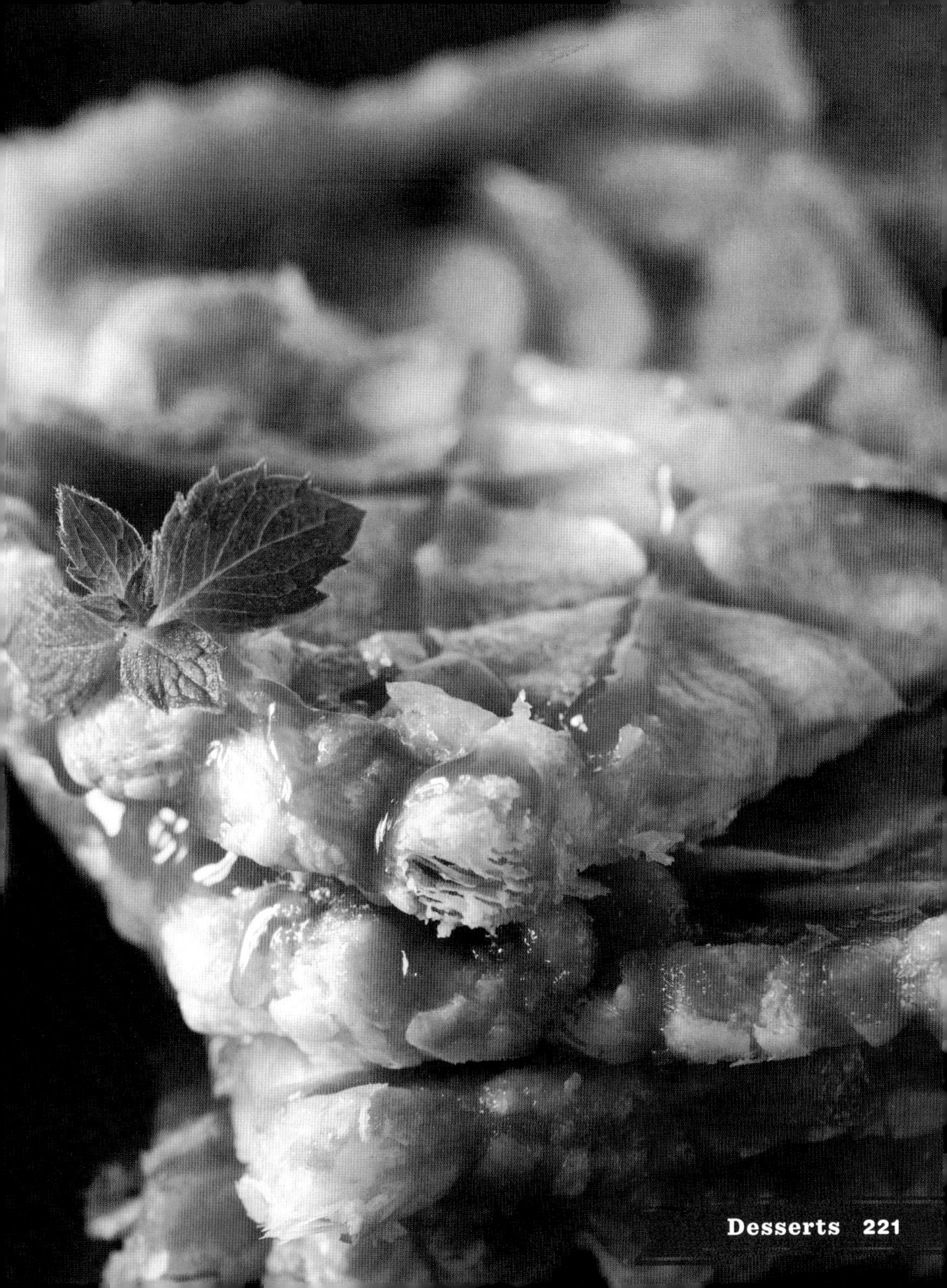

Cookies and Cream Pizza

YIELD: 1 PIZZA • ACTIVE TIME: 20 MINUTES
TOTAL TIME: 1½ HOURS

This recipe is incredibly addictive, so make sure you're very fond of whoever you prepare for it. Chances are, they'll be coming around quite a bit.

1 Place the Oreos in a blender or food processor and process until finely crushed. It is OK if a few large pieces remain. Set aside.

2 Place the cream cheese, sugar, and margarine in a bowl and stir until the ingredients are thoroughly combined and fluffy.

3 Combine pudding and milk in a separate bowl and stir until combined. Stir in the Cool Whip.

4 Add the pudding mixture to the bowl containing the cream cheese mixture. Stir until thoroughly combined. Place the bowl in the refrigerator and chill for at least 1 hour before serving.

5 Preheat the oven to 550°F. When ready, place the pizza in the oven and cook until golden brown, about 10 minutes. Remove from oven and let cool slightly.

6 Remove the mixture from the refrigerator and spread it on the pizza. Sprinkle the Oreo crumbs on top and serve.

INGREDIENTS

1 large package of Oreo cookies

8 oz. cream cheese

1 cup powdered sugar

¼ cup margarine

2 packages of instant vanilla pudding

3½ cups whole milk

12 oz. Cool Whip

1 ball of Basic Pizza Dough (see page 17), stretched into a 10-inch round

Berries, Cherries, and Mascarpone Pizza

**YIELD: 1 PIZZA • ACTIVE TIME: 30 MINUTES
TOTAL TIME: 55 MINUTES**

This is a wonderful dessert for a cool night in the summer, when all of the fruit is in season.

INGREDIENTS

1 ball of Basic Pizza Dough (see page 17), stretched into a 10–inch round

1¼ cups mascarpone cheese

1 pint fresh blueberries

1 pint fresh raspberries

1 cup cherries

Powdered sugar, for topping

1 Preheat the oven to 550°F. When it is ready, place the pizza in the oven and bake until golden brown, about 10 minutes. Remove from oven and let cool slightly.

2 Spread the mascarpone cheese evenly on the cooked pizza crust. Distribute blueberries, raspberries, and cherries as desired. Top with powdered sugar and serve.

Pear, Thyme, Blue Cheese, and Walnut Pizza with Honey

YIELD: 1 PIZZA • ACTIVE TIME: 15 MINUTES
TOTAL TIME: 45 MINUTES

This pizza is savory compared to the rest of the preparations in this chapter, but it's still a very satisfying conclusion to a wonderful meal.

1 Preheat the oven to 550°F. Sprinkle the thyme, blue cheese, and walnuts evenly over the pizza dough.

2 Distribute the pear slices, place in the oven, and cook until the crust is golden brown, about 10 to 15 minutes. Remove, let cool for 5 minutes, and drizzle the honey over the pizza.

INGREDIENTS

2 tablespoons thyme leaves, chopped

1 cup blue cheese, crumbled

1 handful of walnuts

1 ball of Basic Pizza Dough (see page 17), stretched into a 10-inch round

1 pear, cored and sliced

Honey, to taste

Chocolate Hazelnut and Strawberry Pizza

YIELD: 1 PIZZA • ACTIVE TIME: 15 TO 20 MINUTES
TOTAL TIME: 20 TO 30 MINUTES

This homemade version of Nutella is 100 times more flavorful and enchanting. Pizza isn't the only place you'll end up using it.

INGREDIENTS

2 cups hazelnuts

⅓ cup sugar

1 teaspoon sea salt

16 oz. semi–sweet chocolate, chopped

8 tablespoons (1 stick) butter

1 cup heavy cream

1 ball of Basic Pizza Dough (see page 17), stretched into a 10–inch round

2 cups strawberries

1 Preheat the oven to 550°F. Place the hazelnuts in a dry skillet and cook over medium heat until fragrant, approximately 1 minute. Remove hazelnuts from pan and allow to cool. When the hazelnuts are cool, place them in a food processor with the sugar and salt. Pulse until a paste forms.

2 Place the chocolate chips and butter in a microwave–safe bowl and microwave on high in 15–second increments until melted, removing to stir between each increment. When chocolate is melted, remove from heat, add the cream, and whisk until combined. Add hazelnut paste and whisk until thoroughly combined.

3 Once combined, let chill in the refrigerator.

4 Place the pizza in the oven and bake until golden brown, about 10 minutes. Remove from oven and let cool slightly.

5 Spread the hazelnut–and–chocolate mixture on the cooked pizza crust, distribute the strawberries on top, and serve.

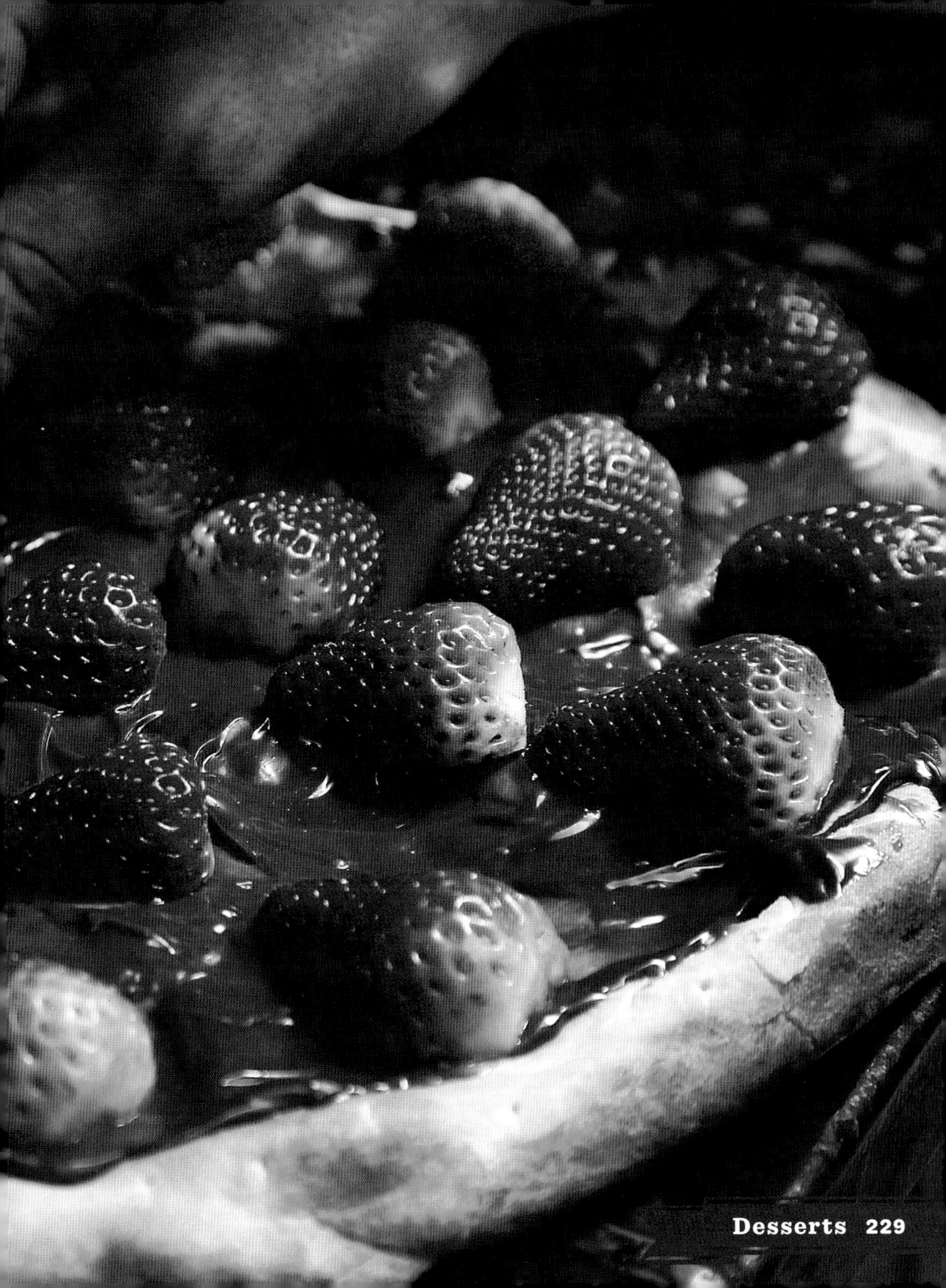

S'mores Pizza

It's common to have a craving for s'mores without a campfire in sight. This delicious pizza allows you to get your fix.

1 Preheat the oven to 550°F. Place the cream cheese, 2 tablespoons of the heavy cream, and the Fluff in a bowl, and beat until fluffy. Fold in the marshmallows and graham cracker crumbs and then set aside.

2 Place the pudding and remaining cream in a separate bowl, stir until combined, and let stand.

3 Place the pizza in the oven and bake until golden brown, about 10 minutes. Remove from oven and let cool slightly.

4 Spread the pudding on the cooked pizza crust. Top with the cream cheese–and–marshmallow mixture and serve.

INGREDIENTS

4 oz. cream cheese

1 cup heavy whipping cream

½ cup Marshmallow Fluff

½ cup miniature marshmallows

¼ cup graham cracker crumbs

¼ cup powdered sugar

½ package of chocolate pudding

1 ball of Basic Pizza Dough (see page 17), stretched into a 10-inch round

Cinnamon Tortillas

YIELD: 6 TO 8 SERVINGS • ACTIVE TIME: 30 MINUTES
TOTAL TIME: 45 MINUTES

You likely have all of these ingredients in the house already. These fantastic little bites will satisfy any sweet tooth.

INGREDIENTS

Vegetable oil

10 Flour Tortillas (see page 88)

1 cup sugar

¼ cup cinnamon

½ teaspoon freshly grated nutmeg

½ teaspoon sea salt

1 Heat 2 inches of vegetable oil in a large saucepan over medium–high heat. When it's hot, drop a handful of the tortillas in and fry for 2 to 3 minutes or until they turn a light golden brown. Remove from oil and dry on a paper towel–lined plate.

2 While tortillas are cooling, combine the sugar, cinnamon, nutmeg, and salt in a bowl. Place the still–warm tortillas in the bowl, toss until coated evenly, and serve.

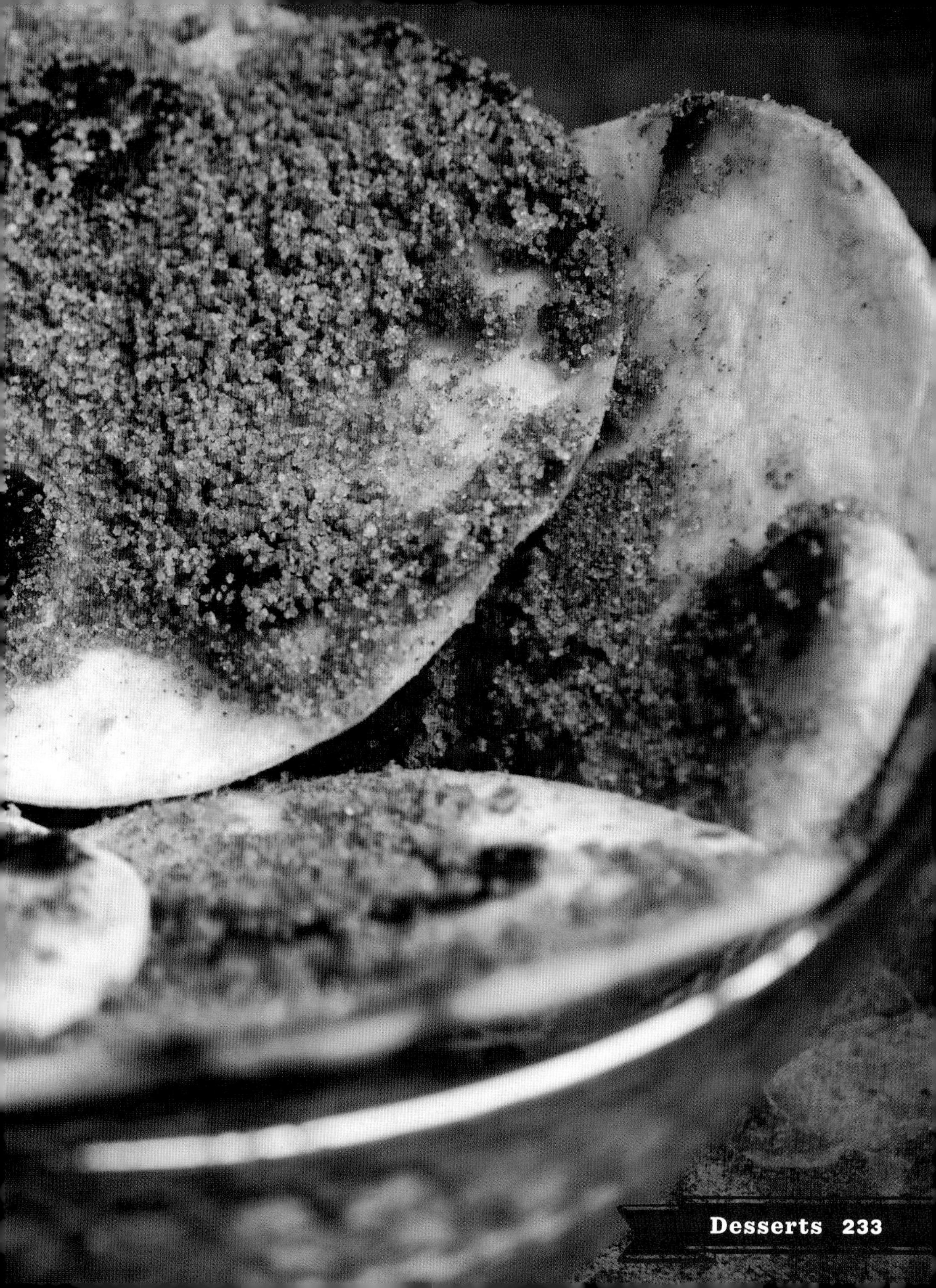

Index

Image Credits

Page 19 courtesy of Pizza Pilgrims

Page 42 courtesy of OTTO Pizza

Page 44 courtesy of Francesco Acri

Pages 55 and 77 courtesy of Theo Kalogeracos

Page 60 courtesy of Alison Mayfield Photography

Pages 71 and 119 courtesy of Barbara Elisi Caracciolo

Page 74 courtesy of Scoozi

Pages 96, 200, and 205 courtesy of Shane Hetherington

Page 140 courtesy of Serena Cosmo

All other images are used under official license from Shutterstock.com.

ABOUT CIDER MILL PRESS BOOK PUBLISHERS

Good ideas ripen with time. From seed to harvest, Cider Mill Press brings fine reading, information, and entertainment together between the covers of its creatively crafted books. Our Cider Mill bears fruit twice a year, publishing a new crop of titles each spring and fall.

"Where Good Books Are Ready for Press"

VISIT US ON THE WEB AT
www.cidermillpress.com

OR WRITE TO US AT
12 Spring Street
PO Box 454
Kennebunkport, Maine 04046